D1546649

Coaching Women
in the Martial Arts

Jennifer Lawler, Ph.D.

MASTERS PRESS

NTC/Contemporary Publishing Group

Library of Congress Cataloging-in-Publication Data

Lawler, Jennifer, 1965–
  Coaching women in the martial arts / Jennifer Lawler.
      p.   cm.
    ISBN 1-57028-211-0
    1. Self-defense for women—Study and teaching. 2. Martial
arts—Study and teaching.   I. Title.
  GV1111.5.L387   1999
  613.7′148′082—dc21

                                    98-42957
                                    CIP

PRAIRIE CREEK PUBLIC LIBRARY DISTRICT
501 Carriage House Lane
Dwight, IL
60420-1399   ILDS #3
TELEPHONE: 815 584-3061
FAX: 815 584-3120

Cover photograph copyright © Bruce Ayres/Tony Stone Images
Cover design by Nick Panos
Interior design by Hespenheide Design
Interior photographs by Jennifer Lawler

Published by Masters Press
A division of NTC/Contemporary Publishing Group, Inc.
4255 West Touhy Avenue, Lincolnwood (Chicago), Illinois 60646-1975 U.S.A.
Copyright © 1999 by Jennifer Lawler

All rights reserved. No part of this book may be reproduced, stored in a
retrieval system, or transmitted in any form or by any means, electronic,
mechanical, photocopying, recording, or otherwise, without the prior permission
of NTC/Contemporary Publishing Group, Inc.

Printed in the United States of America
International Standard Book Number: 1-57028-211-0
  99 00 01 02 03 04 VL 18 17 16 15 14 13 12 11 10 9 8 7 6 5 4 3 2 1

Contents

Coaching Women
in the Martial Arts

Introducing Women to Martial Arts Training

Retaining Female Students

Each year, more and more women sign up for martial arts instruction, for reasons ranging from self-defense to physical fitness. Yet even though most of these women begin their training with enthusiasm, many of them quickly drop out. Although some women quit because of time constraints or incompatible work schedules, the majority of women stop training for less obvious reasons that are therefore harder to address.

External and Internal Conflict

Female martial arts students may encounter negative attitudes from the instructor or other students. They may receive different treatment from male students. They may lack role models in the school. Frequently, these reasons convince women that the martial arts are not, after all, for them. Plenty of external cues suggest that women may not belong.

However, sometimes a woman stops training because of an internal conflict, such as a fear of getting hit or of hitting someone else. So it is important to understand the internal problems a female martial artist faces while at the same time moderating negative external influences.

Unfortunately, many martial arts instructors are not sensitive to the particular needs of female athletes. In fact, many women who begin martial arts training are not especially athletic and therefore are more easily intimidated by the physical demands of the martial arts—even though almost anyone with time, effort, and dedication can acquire the strength, flexibility, and endurance necessary for martial arts performance.

Instructors who are sensitive to the needs of women retain more of their female students and thus become more successful. The key to student retention is in coaching women appropriately. So how can martial arts instructors coach women to achieve the best possible performance? One way is to understand why women join the martial arts and what they expect to get from martial arts training.

Women's Expectations of Training

Perhaps the best way to determine your potential students' goals and expectations is to ask questions when a woman inquires about or signs up for classes. Simply ask why she is thinking about learning the martial arts and what she hopes to get from the experience. This is a good time to encourage her interest while correcting any misconceptions she may have. The martial arts seem slightly sinister to some women. By talking frankly about what and why you teach, you can correct a potential student's misunderstandings. It is also reasonable at this point to explain your expectations as an instructor.

It is also helpful to realize that although women sign up for martial arts instruction for the same reasons (for example, fitness, self-defense) as men, their experiences are very different. Every stage of martial arts training profoundly affects a woman. Although she may sign up because she wants to lose weight, become more fit, or meet new people, she will find herself challenged and inspired at every turn. Martial arts training is nothing like what most women have ever experienced.

The martial arts allow women to experience the exhilaration of physical contact—often for the first time—in a sporting environment. In training, women can feel a sense of control over their own bodies and the excitement of taking care of themselves. This newfound sense of competence and confidence can be empowering. As the instructor, you must remember to respect this, because it is a terrific motivator for women. However, martial arts training can also inhibit women. Most women do not grow up playing sports involving physical contact, and so this first experience with it can be frightening. They are not certain of their bodies' capabilities and worry that they'll hurt themselves—or worse, hurt someone else. And along with the empowerment of martial arts practice comes a responsibility: If I can take care of myself, then it is my obligation—my responsibility—to do so. This responsibility can be a burden in itself, especially for those women who are accustomed to looking to others for security and safety.

Challenges of the Training Hall

The martial arts training hall can be an intimidating place. It is like nowhere else on earth. Some of the rules of conduct in the training hall can be intimidating to women, who tend to have less experience with regimented approaches to teaching and learning. Men are more accustomed to the formality and the hierarchy of martial arts training, and are often even more comfortable wearing a uniform.

Also, women are less accustomed to performing body conditioning exercises like push-ups and sit-ups or crunches. Even physically fit women rarely use calisthenics to build strength and endurance.

Because many women are conditioned to be quiet and not to interrupt people, they are reluctant to kiai (the kiai is a shout that focuses energy). It can be dreadfully embarrassing, especially for a shy woman, to draw attention to herself in this way. One teacher makes it a rule not to pressure students to yell or kiai until it is comfortable for them. Although your impulse might be to insist that your students learn to kiai right away, patience is actually better rewarded in the end.

Because the training hall itself can be intimidating, spend time reviewing the basics of courtesy, discipline, body conditioning, and the like without assuming your students have any previous experience. The easier you make a woman's introduction to the training hall, the more successful her transition will be. Clarifying the rules in the beginning can dramatically ease a new student's anxiety. What may seem perfectly obvious to you is not necessarily apparent to everyone. Remember that women often feel more like outsiders than men—and for good reason. So make the extra effort to seem welcoming to your students.

Adhering to the discipline of the training hall can ultimately be freeing for women. The empowerment that comes from practicing the martial arts is profoundly affecting, but many women are also very disturbed by their new feelings and experiences. Understanding this conflict will help you encourage your students to resolve it.

Benefits of Training

Because martial arts training can be so disconcerting for women, especially at first, it is a good idea to frequently stress its benefits. This can help your students understand what they might experience or encounter in the coming months and years of training. By focusing on the positive—the benefits—you'll encourage students to overcome feelings of doubt and discouragement, and motivate them to continue training.

Often students understand the physical changes that might result from martial arts training. They may wish to become more physically fit, lose weight, or increase their flexibility and power. In addition to becoming stronger and more fit, most students improve their coordination and balance. As these physical changes are taking place, students will become much more aware of themselves and their bodies. This self-knowledge is a pivotal part of the martial arts experience, and it can lead to greater self-understanding and improved self-esteem. Learning to appreciate one's body and what it can do is an exciting aspect of martial arts training.

Other benefits are less obvious to students who first sign up for instruction. For example, although they may think that self-defense training will help prepare them for violence, they may not realize that a side effect of that training is confidence and optimism, even assertiveness. Students feel more confident about standing up for themselves and about taking their place in the world. As a result, martial arts practice can improve self-image and self-esteem, which often fosters self-examination and a greater appreciation of oneself and others.

By preparing women for these changes, an instructor will encourage them to continue their training. Helping students meet the challenges of the martial arts—whether they are physical, mental, or emotional—is an important task for the instructor. These challenges make a person stronger, healthier, and better equipped to function in the world—and the instructor should communicate these benefits to his or her students.

Teaching Women

Teaching Styles

Instructors can best teach their female martial arts students by understanding how people learn. Information is learned in three different ways: through seeing, through hearing, and through physical action. Students should see a technique demonstrated, hear the technique described, and then perform the technique themselves in order for learning to occur at optimum levels. Because different students learn in different ways, all three methods should be used to ensure that all students are reached in one way or another.

How can you use learning styles to help your female students? Because men tend to be more visually oriented, they are more visual learners: seeing a technique demonstrated is often all that is necessary for a male student to understand how to perform it. Women, on the other hand, tend to be more auditory in their learning. That is, they will better understand how to perform a technique by hearing it described. This means that when a teacher demonstrates a technique, he or she should discuss it as well.

Although some martial arts styles call for students to mimic the instructor without any description, discussion, or explanation at all, this is not necessarily the best way to reach all of your students. Instead, talk about the technique as you perform it. Include details, such as how the muscles are working or why the technique is performed. Describe the best way to perform it or how to use it most effectively. Both men and women will benefit if you speak loudly and clearly and repeat your comments a few times. finally, be certain to allow plenty of time for students to practice techniques themselves, particularly under the supervision of an instructor. Physical practice develops "muscle memory." After a number of repetitions (usually several hundred), the martial artist can perform the technique without thinking about it. By incorporating all three ways of learning into your teaching, your students will learn to master the techniques more quickly.

The Learning Process

Several stages are involved in learning each martial arts technique. You should carefully guide this learning process so your students learn the techniques quickly and correctly.

In the first stage, introduce the students to the technique through demonstration and description. If this introduction is performed adequately, students will form a mental picture of a perfectly done technique. This visualization is important for students to internalize knowledge. Next, students should try to do the technique themselves. Most students will be unable to perform the technique perfectly at first, but they will become much more effective with practice and come closer to mastery. After considerable practice, students begin to successfully perform the movement without thinking too much about the details. After training in the technique for some time, the students' physical technique will begin to resemble their perfect mental picture of the technique. This completes the cycle of learning. However, ingraining a physical act so that it becomes almost automatic requires hundreds, if not thousands, of repetitions.

The Instructor's Involvement

For this chain of learning—the learning process—to be effective, the instructor must be closely involved. This involvement consists of four different stages. First, watch the student perform the technique. Second, try to understand what the student is doing and what he or she is attempting to do. (This analysis can be the most difficult part of the teaching process.) Third, explain what the student is doing correctly and incorrectly—information the student needs in order to improve. Finally, after the student has had additional practice, watch the student perform the technique again to see if improvement has occurred. If not, you should demonstrate the technique again, describe how to do it correctly, and allow the student ample time to practice the technique. Then the process of supervision and evaluation begins again.

Women's Expectations of Themselves

While the stages of teaching and learning apply to all students, women students have special needs when learning the martial arts. One teacher says that all of his female students have one thing in common: they are too hard on themselves. They have unrealistically high expectations and expect to achieve perfection too early in the learning process. For instance, they don't think they should fall down when they're performing a spinning wheel kick. The truth of the matter is that everyone falls down doing the spinning wheel kick—at least at first. But sometimes women feel as if they should be able to do techniques perfectly right away.

These high expectations and the subsequent, almost inevitable, feelings of incompetence can complicate martial arts training. They can cause embarrassment, which makes it difficult for the martial artist to practice. Students who feel too self-conscious are less likely to try new and challenging techniques. And feelings of incompetence can cause self-censorship, which causes the martial artist to be inhibited in her performance. Sooner or later, she may conclude that she is a failure at the martial arts and the only solution to this perceived lack of success is to drop out.

Helping Women Learn

Don't let it get this far. Because of their high expectations and sometimes excessive self-criticism, it is important for women to receive plenty of feedback during martial arts training. This helps a woman student to understand that she is on the right track and is making progress toward mastery of the techniques. Offering feedback does not mean you should give praise all of the time or that you need to shout encouragement at every turn. Women do respond to praise and encouragement, but not when it isn't earned. Instead, take the time to explain what your student is doing right. Describe what she could do to make the technique better, but keep these suggestions neutral, not critical. Even if the student isn't performing a technique successfully, encourage her to continue trying. Express your belief that she will master the technique eventually, if she gives it enough time, effort, and practice.

Avoid Advice Overload

It is also important to realize that although women are good at listening and learning, too often they are overloaded with advice from others. This is because they're polite and patient and will listen to what others have to say. This "advice overload" can lead to frustration.

One student recalls the time when she was learning how to do a spinning wheel kick. As she practiced with different partners during class, she was told to envision herself picking up a quarter, to keep her leg stiff as a board, to imagine someone pulling her shoulder down, and a number of other analogies. She became so overwhelmed by the different suggestions that she couldn't do the kick at all. When she asked the head instructor for help, he realized that she didn't need any more advice. She just needed to keep practicing. After practicing on her own for a few class sessions, she was able to do the kick successfully. Sometimes a student simply needs to practice without any input from others.

Problems with High Expectations

Because of her high expectations, a woman might be embarrassed when she can't do a new technique perfectly right away. Because it takes considerable practice to become proficient in martial arts techniques, a women might become frustrated. So she might say, "I'm having trouble with my jump kick," or whatever the technique is. This doesn't necessarily mean that there is a problem or that you need to solve her problem. She is just expressing self-doubt. Sometimes all you have to do is simply validate her experience. Therefore, an appropriate reply to "I'm having trouble with this kick" is "It is a tough kick, but you'll get it." This shows that you understand that she is trying and that you are encouraging her persistence. Even if she asks for advice, try to withhold making immediate comments. Stand by and watch her do her technique several times before offering any advice—and then, remember to point out what she is doing right.

So one key to teaching women is to understand what they need—and not to talk too much. Martial arts are learned through physical practice, not through continuous discussion.

Women's Ways of Learning

Because women learn differently than men, at least to some extent, they will challenge your teaching in different ways. For example, women tend to be much more inquisitive than men. A man in a formal, regimented class is more likely to do as he is told without questioning it. Although a woman will hold her tongue, she'll have plenty of questions to ask when she's allowed. This means she'll ask you why you do certain techniques, and she'll ask you if it wouldn't be better to do a different technique. She may ask you why you do a certain technique differently than another instructor. This curiosity is not meant to challenge the teacher's authority. It is simply a matter of differing experiences. Because more men participate in organized sports and the like, they tend to be more comfortable in the traditional training hall, with its highly structured approach and its discouragement of questions.

But the fact that women may be more curious does not mean that you should allow or encourage women to speak up in class if you don't normally do so. (It also doesn't mean that you should reprimand them when they do.) It simply means that you should make the rules of the class clear from the beginning and ask students to keep their questions for break time or for after class. Be patient with questions and challenges. The more a woman understands the underlying reasons for certain actions, the greater the likelihood that she'll cooperate and grow in the martial arts. Satisfying her curiosity encourages her to continue with her training.

Cooperative Learning

To promote learning, encourage your students to work with each other. This will help everyone become better martial artists in the long run. The teaching and learning that takes place among martial arts partners cannot be duplicated in any other way. If one student asks another why a certain technique is done, it requires the other student to know more about martial arts than if they were never asked such questions. Further, many women enjoy helping others or working with partners to improve their skills. But it is important for this environment to be encouraging. Set guidelines for working with partners and remind students of those guidelines periodically.

When women work with partners, emphasize cooperation, not competition. Instead of competing with her partner to see who can kick higher (although this can be fun to do sometimes), a female martial artist is more likely to be interested in working with her partner so that each can learn how to kick as high as possible. This is usually a more satisfying approach for women. Therefore, try to downplay competition among students while emphasizing individual achievement.

Women's Alternative Approaches

Keep in mind that many women approach problems differently. Men tend to take a direct, linear approach to any subject or problem. They will keep trying something in a certain way—perhaps a way that they have been shown is successful—until they succeed. For example, a man may continue to hit a heavy bag over and over and over until he feels he is hitting it with enough power. A woman, on the other hand, may attempt to hit the heavy bag a few times. If she doesn't succeed in demonstrating enough power, she may feel she should modify her technique and try a different approach. This doesn't mean that she's giving up. It simply means that she's seeking an alternative way of doing something.

Responding to Alternative Approaches

You can respond to a student who pursues alternative approaches in several ways. You can encourage her to continue practicing the new technique without changing her approach, perhaps by setting a number of times you would like her to do the technique. You might say, "Don't stop until you have done this fourteen times." At the end of that practice session, she should feel stronger and more powerful. She can demonstrate this by showing the technique to you.

Alternatively, you can allow her to perform a few tries while you are watching. Then you can discuss what she could do differently to generate more power. You might also encourage her to follow her instincts and try an alternative way of generating power on her own, without your advice. But be sure to check with her periodically so that she doesn't end up doing a technique incorrectly. Your recognition that women seek alternative ways of solving problems will prevent you from misinterpreting their motives.

Women's Self-Perception

As an instructor, you may be surprised when a female student doesn't seem to be able to follow your commands. For example, you may say, "Lower your front stance." If she doesn't respond appropriately, you may further explain, "Bend your front knee more." Still you may find that she has trouble doing as you ask. But this seeming inability to follow your commands doesn't necessarily mean she does not understand what you are saying or asking of her. In fact, she may not be completely in touch with the way her body works. She may think she is doing as you ask, but because she is so disconnected from her body, her thought and the physical expression of it do not match.

Unfortunately, few women reach adulthood without having a distorted view of their own bodies. This can make it very difficult for them to perform physically. When one is completely estranged from one's body—has even been taught to hate it—it can be very difficult to regain command over it and learn how it works, what it really looks like, and what it can do.

Correcting Distorted Perception

One the most important things a martial arts instructor can do is to help his or her female students see their bodies accurately. This should be a completely neutral exercise. It shouldn't be about whether the student is big or small or tall or short. It should simply be about helping her to understand her body and how it works. Because their view of their bodies is so distorted, practicing in front of mirrors is essential for good martial arts performance for women.

As a helpful exercise, stand beside the student and first perform the technique yourself. Then have her perform it. Finally, perform the technique simultaneously with her, explaining what you are doing and what you see the student doing. Feel free to touch the student to correct her technique, but be certain to do this in a neutral, professional way. By practicing with you, she will come to see what her own body is doing and can better control it in the future.

Another approach is to physically fix or correct her techniques. For instance, guide her arm as she blocks so that she knows how the block should be done. Fix the angle of her hand if she strikes incorrectly. This physical correction—done in a neutral, professional way—helps the student *feel* how to do the technique correctly.

Avoiding Stereotypes

Understanding the special needs of women can help you meet their needs better. By the same token it is important to avoid preconceived ideas about women. Although this book discusses teaching women in general, and is meant to help you form a female-friendly school and a female-friendly teaching philosophy, remember that all women are individuals. Some women are perfectly comfortable in a martial arts environment, although many are not. Not all women are emotional or weak or talkative, although some might be. Some women are competitive, athletic, and outgoing. Other women are not. But most women do not like being victims, do not like being quiet, and do not like being passive. The martial arts help them to overcome these problems, and you can be an important part of that process. But it is essential that you see your female students as students first, with individual needs, abilities, problems, talents, and skills.

Fear

Women's Expression of Fear

Many women approach the martial arts with a number of different fears. They bring with them to the training hall a fear of being hurt, a fear of hurting someone else, even a fear of falling. They may be afraid of their own violence. They may be afraid of their own feelings when they work out. You must remember that your female students come from an environment that expects women to be weak, frightened, and insecure.

Women express their fears in different ways. They won't necessarily cry or readily admit they are afraid. Often a woman expresses her fear by disengaging. She will back away—even physically—in order to gain control over her fear. For example, during one-steps or sparring practice she may be afraid of falling or of being thrown to the floor. Because of this fear, she may step away from her partner, making it difficult for her partner to practice the technique. In addition, if she is not confident of her own techniques, she may apologize for them. She may ask for advice and help. She may do many things to avoid actually having to perform the technique. This disengagement is one expression of fear.

Another way fear is communicated is through overanalysis, or simply too much talking. For example, one student has never liked sparring. Whenever she spars with a partner, she will do one or two techniques and then stop. She will discuss sparring. She will describe what her partner is doing. She will encourage her partner to try different techniques. She will overanalyze the match and delay the sparring as long as possible. Then she'll do another technique and stop, and another discussion ensues. This is not helpful for the student or for her partners. Unfortunately, this kind of disengagement is a very common occurrence, and, sadly, it doesn't help the woman overcome her fears.

You must intervene early in training to address such expressions of fear. Sometimes it is simply a matter of starting very slowly. Sometimes it is a matter of drawing the student's attention to what she's doing. Devoting time and attention to helping women face their fears instead of disengaging from them is well worth the effort.

Fear of Hitting and of Being Hit

The fears that a woman brings with her to the martial arts must be addressed for her to continue training. In this case, my own experience has always guided me. When I began my training in the martial arts, I was a twenty-something, middle-class, well-educated woman. I had never faced an act of violence in my life, unless you count getting elbowed while standing in line for tickets to a Beach Boys concert. I was fascinated by the martial arts and enjoyed my training, but I was afraid of two things: I was afraid of hitting and I was afraid of getting hit.

My fears made it difficult to spar. I would stand three or four feet away from my partner and do my techniques to the air. Once, when a partner made contact with my thigh, I went to the locker room and cried. I have never been an emotional person and it bothered me to be so upset. I told one of the other martial artists that I had been hit and it had hurt and that bothered me. Instead of dismissing my concern, the woman—a black belt—spoke to the head instructor and told him what I'd said. In subsequent classes, the instructor reminded all students not to make contact when sparring with students at my level. I was a little self-conscious because I was afraid everyone would know that I was the one who had complained, but mostly I was relieved and pleased. I felt like my concern had been legitimate and that it had been heard. This made me more confident. It was clear that the instructor didn't want me to get hurt and would try to prevent it, and this was very reassuring to me.

The female black belt who had listened to my concern about getting hit also encouraged me to learn how to hit her. It was a horrible thing to learn. I was terrified. It was worse than being hit myself. Hitting other people is not something that nice middle-class women do. I felt violated when I hit somebody else. But this black belt helped me to see it in a neutral way. I was simply sparring. There was neither good nor bad attached to it; it simply was. She would often stand there and tell me to come closer and closer. Then she would tell me to strike with a punch or kick. She would encourage me to continue coming closer and closer until I touched her uniform. Her incredible patience enabled me to learn how to hit other people—which is, of course, a very important part of sparring practice. I even learned how to be hit myself. Now my favorite part of martial arts training is sparring practice. This never would have been possible without the patience of my remarkable mentor.

Particularly for self-defense, women must learn how to hit and how to be hit. If you learn that you can get hit pretty hard without permanent damage, being struck won't completely demoralize you when someone threatens you with violence. Although it is absolutely essential to teach a woman how to hit and how to be hit, sometimes it must be done slowly and carefully. Students can practice with targets until they're comfortable striking people (Figure 1–1).

Figure 1-1
Have new students practice kicking targets if they're uncomfortable striking people.

a

b

c

Introducing Women to the Martial Arts

One of the best ways to introduce a woman to the martial arts and to encourage her to continue is to begin slowly and personally. Suggest a few private lessons at first, or at least encourage her to attend a small class. This personal attention in the begining will assuage her feelings of confusion and frustration; she will be less flustered and more interested in pursuing the martial arts. The first few lessons are the most important in martial arts training, so be certain they are done correctly.

It is also important for her to learn some skills that she can immediately apply to her life. Although we understand that martial arts mastery takes years, even decades, tools and skills taught at the beginning enable women to see the empowering side of the martial arts. In my school, students are taught to do a sidekick right away. Within the first week or two, they are encouraged to break a board with the sidekick. Their success makes them feel strong and powerful, and they realize they can become stronger and more powerful in many different ways if they continue their martial arts training. This motivational tool convinces many students that everything that follows is worthwhile—including the cuts, the bruises, the exhaustion, the muscle cramps, and the frustration. Nothing compares to the validation of your decision to study the martial arts.

2

ATTITUDES WOMEN ENCOUNTER IN THE TRAINING HALL

Not long ago, a martial arts magazine ran the following headline on its cover: "Do Women Belong in the Martial Arts?" That, unfortunately, is an attitude women encounter all too frequently in the training hall. If you or any of your students have asked yourselves this question, perhaps you should consider why you have such an attitude; you should also be aware of its negative consequences.

Another martial arts magazine proudly proclaims that it profiles female martial artists. But to be considered for this profile, female martial artists must submit a full-length photo of themselves in a swimsuit. It is very unlikely that male martial artists are expected to do the same. But such an attitude—that women in martial arts are flattered to be considered sex objects—can be very discouraging.

The attitudes that women encounter in the training hall (and outside it) have a great deal to do with whether they pursue martial arts training. Although you cannot control the outside world, you can control what goes on in the training hall. If you treat your female students as equals to your male students, they'll respect you and probably continue training under your tutelage. In other words, if you maintain a gender-neutral environment, you'll be much more likely to retain your female students. Expecting the same effort from all your students doesn't mean you should ignore the particular needs of women, just that you believe they share the interests and abilities of your male students.

If you want to attract and keep female students, you must remember that you are the ultimate role model for all of your students. That is, your students learn from you how to behave toward women. You will need to instill in students the values that you believe are important. In a female-friendly school, these values include a respect for women and their abilities.

Negative Attitudes

Even in a training hall that promotes equality, women will occasionally encounter men who have a negative attitude toward them or their abilities. It is important for you to discourage such attitudes—not only with words, but also with actions. If you learn that a student is disparaging another student, it is important for you to address this. Nothing ruins the morale and environment of a school faster than someone who treats others badly. You might speak with the offender in private or you might discuss attitudes in general during class. If you don't feel comfortable drawing attention to the specifics of a problem—"some of you have a bad attitude toward women"—you should explain that negative attitudes toward others represents poor etiquette. You can also supervise the offending student more closely in order to prevent such negative attitudes from being expressed.

Lack of Cooperation

The negative attitudes women encounter can seem minor, but they are nonetheless very frustrating. One way that some men express negativism is by refusing to cooperate. For instance, one male student would always make it difficult for lower-belt women to throw him. He didn't do this with men or with women who had confidence and a higher rank. This refusal to cooperate—along with a mean-spirited desire to slight his partners—made a lot of women dislike him enormously. They didn't want to work with him, and his childish behavior poisoned the entire atmosphere.

A negative attitude expressed as a lack of cooperation is a very common problem. This is especially hard on women who need confidence and encouragement in the beginning stages of training.

Belittling Others

Some men may belittle the efforts of female students. They might say something like, "You'll never be strong enough to do that kick." Or they will constantly criticize what their female partner is doing. She isn't performing a technique correctly, or she isn't holding the target right. One student used to tell women that they actually hindered his progress because he couldn't practice his kicks as hard with them as he could with men. His instructor would remind him that a heavy bag, not a human partner, was designed to take the brunt of his full power.

Other Negative Expressions

Sometimes negativity is expressed in even more subtle ways. A male student may simply sigh when he's assigned a female partner. Or he may do something a little childish, such as not holding a target correctly or ignoring his partner's efforts when others are encouraging their partners.

One student consistently worked with women in a lazy way. If he was supposed to hold a target, he'd let it hang about knee high. If his female partner asked him to raise the target higher so that she could kick the appropriate height, he would say something like, "You can't kick that high anyway." Because his attitude was not corrected, an unpleasant incident occurred when he failed to hold a target correctly for a female black belt. When he refused to raise the target, she blasted a kick as hard as she could at his knees (which was where he was holding the target), causing him to fall and injure himself. If his negative attitude had been addressed earlier, and in an appropriate way, such a retaliation would never have happened. Of course, after this incident the student started holding the target correctly and learned to keep his thoughts to himself.

All such behavior, although subtle, is unacceptable. Passive negativity is difficult to deal with but must be addressed in order to maintain a positive, friendly training hall.

Discussing Courtesy

Generally, passive negative behavior and subtle negative attitudes can be handled with discussions of courtesy. Counsel students that negative or biased opinions must not be expressed in the training hall. Punish a student with twenty push-ups every time he or she displays a negative attitude. This will show not only the student in question but other students as well that you expect cooperation and courtesy in your training hall. Keep the discussion professional and describe what you want to see—full cooperation with all partners—and what you don't want to see—disrespectful behavior in any form.

Bullying Behavior

Sometimes the negative attitudes a woman might encounter are expressed in more serious ways. Unfortunately, a number of men think they have something to prove to women. They may spar harder than they should. They may throw a woman to the mat with excessive violence. This bullying attitude is frequently displayed toward women who are just beginning training—bullies don't pick on people their own size, so men and higher-ranking women aren't usually their targets. A woman who is subject to aggressive physical displays, especially as a beginner, has a good reason to quit training.

Because bullies tend to be more physical in expressing their negative attitudes, they can be dangerous liabilities in the training hall. It is important to stop such aggressive behavior immediately. This means you must be vigilant in supervising your classes. A person who is aggressive with one partner is often aggressive with others. Because of the physical nature of his negative attitude, this type of person can cause injury as well as upset.

A bully must be disciplined appropriately. A sternly worded reprimand and close supervision are necessary. If this does not solve the problem, the student may have to be asked to leave the school before he drives off or seriously injures other students.

Gender-Oriented Attitudes

Nice Guy, Misguided Attitude

Although negative attitudes are unpleasant, they are relatively easy to identify, and you can take action to keep these attitudes and their expression in check. More common and more difficult to identify and treat is the attitude that focuses unnecessary attention on a woman's gender. This is an attitude that many very nice men happen to have. For example, if they are sparring a woman and her uniform top slides open, they can become very embarrassed. They'll stop sparring and apologize, or make an issue of allowing the woman to adjust her uniform. This is because they perceive their sparring partner as a woman and not simply as a sparring partner. In some ways, this problem is the opposite of the negative attitudes women often encounter. In this case, the other students are trying to be too considerate of the female students. Sometimes while grappling or throwing, a male partner might accidentally touch his female partner's chest. This can be very embarrassing for the male partner. Again, he may stop what he's doing. He may apologize profusely.

The problem with this attitude is that it focuses too much attention on the female partner's gender. If you're sparring a woman, or grappling with a woman, or throwing a woman, her uniform top will occasionally pop open, or you'll occasionally touch her breast. This happens and is nothing to be embarrassed about. No one's dignity has suffered an irreparable slight. But it is very hard to convince some men of this.

But this type of attitude is difficult to address. What are you going to say? Announce to your classes that it's okay to see a woman's sports bra? The best approach for these situations is simply to make certain that all of your male students practice with female partners repeatedly so that they become used to working with women. They will, over time, begin to treat their female partners like any other partner.

It helps if your female students can maintain their sense of humor. One woman recalls a partner who always got embarrassed when they sparred. Things she didn't consider any big deal really embarrassed him. (As she said, if you're going to allow punches to the chest, you're occasionally going to punch a woman's breast. It's nothing to worry about.) But her partner's embarrassment would be contagious and after a while she would get embarrassed. This inhibited both of them and made it very difficult for them to practice. She tried not reacting, but this further embarrassed her partner, who thought she was either mad at him or acting stoic, so finally she decided to try humor. The next time something happened that embarrassed her partner, she said, "Now how are you going to tell your wife about that?" For some reason, this approach worked and both partners were able to relax, enjoy their martial arts practice, and not get embarrassed. Any method that can diffuse an embarrassing situation is worth trying.

This misguided attitude can be expressed in other ways. Sometimes a man, overly concerned with the fact that his partner is a woman, will attempt to encourage or compliment her by saying, "You're as good as a man." Such comments can be very annoying to women, because it implies that being a woman is not good enough. A comment like this is not usually meant in a malicious way. In fact, the male student is trying to express appreciation of the female student's abilities. Rather than being mean-spirited, such remarks are often just a little misguided.

There is not much you can do about the attitude that leads to such remarks, except be certain that you never make remarks like this yourself. When one instructor hears such comments, he responds to the man, "And you're as fast as a woman." If you feel you should say something, keep it light and instructive.

Unwanted Interest

On occasion, a male student may make an unwanted advance to a female student. (This will happen whenever men and women get together in the same room for any length of time.) However, in the school where I train, three couples have met and married in the last few years. Obviously not all advances are unwanted, so bans on dating among students or other drastic policies are probably not the answer. But if you overhear an unwanted advance, or if a student complains about unwanted advances, you should respond appropriately. (Of course, women can pursue uninterested men, too; they should be handled the same way that you would handle a persistent male admirer.)

If the advances persist, you should explain firmly to the offending individual that such behavior does not belong in the training hall. You can limit his contact with the object of his affection by being certain not to pair the two in class together. You might also involve him before and after classes with other activities, such as supervising another student's forms practice, to reduce the chance of his bothering other people.

Encourage your female students, if they've complained, to simply and firmly turn him down. Without their help, this situation may be more difficult for you to stop. Any woman who is approached by the student in question shouldn't offer excuses or apologies—she should simply say no. Otherwise, he may continue with his persistence in the mistaken belief that sooner or later the woman he is pursuing will agree to see him romantically.

You may need to ask a truly persistent man to leave the school, because his unwelcome behavior can affect the whole environment and drive off students.

Creating a Positive Atmosphere

Most of the negative attitudes women encounter in the training hall have to do with respect (or, rather, the lack of respect). While you cannot force students to respect one another, you can expect them to be courteous. By enforcing guidelines for courtesy, you can avoid overt displays of negative, unwanted attitudes. Your insistence will instill the importance of keeping the environment positive and supportive. Over time, students who are expected to be courteous to one another also learn to respect the skills and abilities of their classmates.

One way to foster a better attitude and a positive atmosphere in your training hall is to remove or downplay the focus on competition. If you focus more on cooperation and learning as opposed to comparison and competition, you'll find that a healthier attitude prevails. There is really no need for winners and losers all the time, particularly in martial arts training. A spirit of cooperation is one of the best ways to improve attitudes and to reduce the expression of negativity.

3
Fostering a Winning Spirit

A good martial arts school fosters a sense of school spirit, community, and teamwork. With the right attitude, a student in a good martial arts school will learn that he or she can do anything. This belief is called "winning spirit" or "indomitable spirit." It is not about winning or losing, but instead about approaching training with a serious mindset and with the intention to work hard to become a better martial artist.

What a Winning Spirit Means

I once hurt myself during a tae kwon do class. My physician told me that people who play martial arts often get this type of injury. I was surprised when I heard him use the word *play* to describe what I do. I've never thought of myself—or any other martial artist—as *playing* martial arts. We *practice* the martial arts. And that's an entirely different thing. It means that we're not perfect—that we have not completely mastered the skills. It means that it is not a sport with winners and losers. It also means that we take the martial arts seriously, that we aren't "playing" at them. Practicing the martial arts is much like practicing an instrument. It is an art. To "play" a martial art seems to indicate a lack of seriousness, a lack of purpose. In fact, it is this serious intention that helps the student develop a winning spirit.

Developing winning spirit does not depend on winning. Each student must cultivate a winning spirit to become a better martial artist and consequently a better person. As the instructor, it is up to you to give your students the tools they need to develop a winning spirit.

The Five Elements of Teaching

The best way to help your students develop a winning spirit is to remember and practice the five elements of teaching. By doing so, you will guide your students in the appropriate direction.

The first element of teaching is to develop a relationship of *trust* with your students. This means that they have to believe that you have their best interests at heart. They won't believe this if you are constantly late for class, forget your promises, or increase tuition every other month. But a trusting relationship also means that you can expect your students to do their best at all times. It means that when they enter the training hall, they are prepared for practice—not distracted by the events of the day or too tired to perform adequately.

The second element of teaching is setting reasonable, clear *expectations* for your students. This means that when they take a promotion test they should know what they will have to do. Of course this does not mean you can't challenge or surprise them. In fact, facing challenges and confronting the unexpected are essential to martial arts training. But for the most part, it should be clear what you expect your students to be able to do. Those expectations should be reasonable and attainable for anyone who puts forth a serious effort.

The third element of teaching is explaining the *purpose* of each aspect of the martial art that you teach. For example, explain why doing forms is important to the martial artist. In addition to teaching balance, grace, and coordination, you may have personal reasons why you think forms training is important. Be certain you explain this to your students. Explaining the purpose of each of the different techniques that you teach enables your students to use them appropriately, apply them to the correct situation, and become smarter martial artists.

The fourth element of teaching is fostering *consistency* in your teaching. This means that if it is wrong to talk in class, it should always be wrong to talk in class. If people who are late to class aren't allowed to participate, no exceptions should be made. If you expect your students to bow to senior belts, then all students should bow to all senior belts. With consistency comes discipline, which is an important component of the martial arts. If you have assistant instructors, their teaching should be consistent with your methods. They should be encouraged to model their techniques after yours. An assistant instructor who does a front kick differently from you will confuse your students. If it's okay to talk in the assistant's class but not in yours, students will get a mixed message about what is important and what is expected of them.

The fifth element of teaching is offering *encouragement* to your students. Encouragement is necessary to the development of martial artists. Otherwise they may become discouraged and drop out. But encouragement and praise must be earned to be appropriate—and to be appreciated. Don't give out praise and encouragement too lavishly. Reserve it for those times when it is actually deserved. Your students will sense that your comments are sincere and they will respond more enthusiastically.

Strength and Power

Understanding Strengths

Fostering a winning spirit in your students, especially your female students, means helping them to capitalize on their strengths. When a person feels competent, she performs better, has a better experience, and demonstrates a better attitude. Like self-esteem, a winning spirit is not something you can give to your students; it is something they must earn. But as an instructor, you can give your students the opportunities and the guidance necessary for them to develop winning spirit. Therefore, help your students achieve competence by focusing on their strengths.

One of the most obvious strengths of women is flexibility. For example, although a female student might be shorter than a male student, her flexibility might enable her to kick higher.

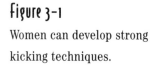

Figure 3-1

Women can develop strong kicking techniques.

Therefore, you should encourage her to attempt techniques that take advantage of her flexibility.

By the same token, women tend to be stronger in their lower bodies than in their upper bodies. This means that they should focus on learning and using their legs and hips, as in kicking techniques (Figure 3–1). Playing to their obvious advantages helps them to feel competent and powerful.

Understanding Power

In addition, remind your female students that power is not simply a matter of mass or weight. Women often feel overpowered by bigger men. Remind your female students that power is an equation derived by multiplying speed with mass or weight. Therefore, a faster person can be just as powerful as a heavier person (Figure 3–2). Teaching your female students to cultivate speed techniques makes them as powerful as any big man.

a

Figure 3-2
Techniques don't have to rely on muscle and mass to be effective.

b

c

Increasing Power

You can encourage female students to develop strength and power in other ways as well. Because of their different anatomies, women tend to have much weaker upper bodies than men. But they can compensate for this with weight training or practicing other strengthening techniques. They don't necessarily need to start a weight training regimen; you can show your female students simple ways to improve their strength. For example, you can encourage them to box or punch a heavy bag. This is a wonderful way to develop a stronger upper body.

Be certain to demonstrate correct boxing or punching techniques. Show them how to use their whole body weight behind a punch or hand strike. This will help them realize how powerful they can be. If you encourage your female students to punch a heavy bag for just fifteen minutes after class every other day, they will find themselves much stronger—and stronger more quickly—than they would have imagined possible.

Conversely, some women are unaware of their own power. Because they have been taught to view themselves as weak, passive, and powerless, women can be oblivious to their own strength.

This is the case with one student who is very big and powerful. Whenever she spars with anyone smaller, she frequently kicks or punches much too hard. On several occasions she has caused her partners enough pain to make them quit the match; she has even caused a minor injury or two. She is always flustered and apologetic after this happens. She is not a bully, nor is she trying to prove anything. She's simply much, much stronger than she thinks she is.

Learning About Power

Several methods can help a strong student realize how much power she possesses. For example, assign the student to a heavy bag and show her how hard she strikes. This contact with a solid object may help her to understand her strength. Have some other students strike the heavy bag so that she can compare herself with them.

Another method to help her understand control and contact involves a small padded target or focus mitt. Have her practice barely touching the target even when she's at full extension with her techniques.

A powerful person who doesn't realize her strength may also need to work on pulling her techniques, so that when she touches another person she does not continue to follow through. Sometimes people who are big and strong have trouble stopping themselves once they've committed themselves to performing a technique—the momentum keeps them going. Practice in pulling their punches and kicks will help prevent injury to a partner. Sometimes a student simply needs to learn to stop the technique as soon as it touches her partner.

By helping your female students understand power and how it is achieved, and by showing them how to take advantage of their natural abilities, you will help them feel competent and confident. This inspires a winning spirit.

Self-Confidence

Discourage Comparison

Another key to fostering a winning spirit is to encourage your students not to compare themselves too much with others. It is good to have role models. Many women improve their techniques by watching others. But this can also be discouraging. We can't all be eighteen, slender, and flexible forever. Encourage your students to see the positive in who they are. A forty-year-old woman who has had three children isn't as quick as an eighteen-year-old—but she might discover that she's very powerful. Or she might realize that she is extremely smart—and a smart martial artist can overcome a powerful one anytime. A student's goal should be to become the best martial artist she can be. This goal cannot be reached through constant comparison. Unfortunately, many women are conditioned to compare themselves to others, so you may have to actively encourage your female students to find their own strengths and abilities.

Another reason to discourage comparison is that we often shortchange others when we compare ourselves with them. Perhaps we think that their techniques are sloppy or they demonstrate very little power. Although this may be true, it is not a good attitude to take. And we often communicate our negative judgments of another student without realizing it. No matter how they are expressed, negative judgments about one's performance can be discouraging.

Remind your students to look at themselves first. We can all use a little improvement. Only when instructing another person and helping them to improve is it really necessary to judge them. Therefore, encourage your students to reserve judgment of others. Remind them to work on their own performance by keeping the competition to a minimum. This develops a winning spirit that permeates the entire training hall. In the martial arts, a true winning spirit is built on the continual attempt to do your best. It has little to do with how others around you perform.

Developing Self-Confidence

One of the most important elements of doing one's best is developing enough self-confidence to trust oneself. This is sometimes difficult for female martial artists who lack previous athletic experience. They're not as in touch with their bodies, they're often afraid for themselves and for others. Even athletic women don't often participate in sports with physical contact. Men, even those who have no experience in organized sports such as football, are more likely to have played rough games or have gotten into fistfights when they were young. For women, this lack of previous experience makes the physical contact of the martial arts a frightening thing.

Helping your female students to overcome these fears will enable them to cultivate a winning spirit. Teach them that being in the proper frame of mind and trying to appear confident is helpful. Often if we can learn not to *act* afraid we can learn not to *be* afraid.

Confidence

Confidence that comes from simple physical practice helps to develop winning spirit. Confident students are more likely to practice martial arts with enthusiasm and skill. Confidence can be nurtured by setting goals that are challenging but not impossible to achieve. You can begin by setting these goals yourself, but as your students become more confident, they can set their own goals. To help them set their own goals in the beginning, consider their skills and what they should be able to accomplish. For example, suppose a female student is just learning how to do forms. Have her goal be to do her form completely, without stopping, with no hesitation and no mistakes. Explain that you don't expect her to do the form perfectly, but that you want her to be able to do the form from beginning to end smoothly without stopping to think about what comes next.

Other goals can be set when the student is learning how to spar. Set her a goal of blocking at least two techniques per match. She may not be able to do this right away, but she can achieve this goal pretty quickly. Then make the goal more challenging. Have her try to score at least one unblocked point on each opponent she faces.

By setting challenging, achievable goals, you make your student feel more confident in her skills. You also help her focus on one or two things at a time, instead of having her scatter her energy trying to do everything perfectly right away. Soon your student will be able to understand enough about the art that she is practicing to set her own goals. Her commitment to achieving these goals will be a manifestation of a true winning spirit.

Fostering a Winning Spirit in the Training Hall

Other qualities are necessary to develop a winning spirit as well. Creating an environment where ego is not supreme is essential. Insisting that students treat one another with respect and honesty is important. Encouraging perseverance, which requires students to keep trying, can help them achieve things that seemed impossible. Teaching restraint can help students to control both the body and emotions. This control means that they won't use emotions such as fear and anger to make decisions. And the right attitude—an attitude of positive optimism regardless of whether we win or lose—is essential to success in the training hall (as well as in life).

Guidelines for Conduct

As an instructor, it is up to you to establish guidelines for conduct. In most styles in the martial arts, students are expected to cultivate certain personal qualities that are thought to improve character. Tae kwon do has the *five tenets*. Different karate styles have special codes of conduct. Make sure you understand and communicate these guidelines to your students. Help them understand what they mean.

Tae kwon do students are introduced to the five tenets as white belts. They are expected to memorize them. (The five tenets are courtesy, integrity, perseverance, self-control, and indomitable spirit.) As students progress through the ranks, they are expected to define what each of the qualities means. As beginning martial arts students, their definitions of the five tenets are literal and easy to understand. They may simply say that courtesy, for example, means being nice and respectful to other people.

As students continue their progress, they are asked to describe how each quality is expressed in the training hall. At this point, they may say that courtesy is expressed by bowing to the senior belts.

Finally, as students approach the higher levels of the colored belt ranks, they are expected to demonstrate how the five tenets apply to everyday life. Students are also asked how they practice each tenet. They may reply that they are more polite to their spouses and that they try to get along better with their bosses. In this way, they are expected to learn the five tenets and to incorporate them into all aspects of their lives.

Some Japanese-style schools teach students to be *resolute in five respects*. These are five commitments to training that all martial artists must make. These commitments require perseverance, determination, and a winning spirit. To become resolute in five respects, students should believe in the philosophy of the school, stay fit regardless of personal circumstances, be committed to mastering the skills they are shown, be willing to participate in arduous training, and do their best in competition. Following such guidelines can make a student a superior martial artist and a better person. Such rules of conduct are essential to developing a true winning spirit.

Chi and Winning Spirit

Certain mental attitudes are necessary to cultivate a winning spirit. These mental attitudes are described in different ways, but focus and determination are usually considered to be the keys. To give one's best effort and to achieve one's martial arts goals—thereby cultivating a winning spirit—the martial artist must have focus and determination.

Most martial arts teach concepts such as *chi*, which is simply the life force or vital energy that all things possess. In traditional martial arts, it is believed that chi is located in the abdomen and that it can be controlled through breathing. Martial artists attempt to summon chi by using shouts or kiai. It is believed that using chi makes a person more powerful than using physical strength alone.

For modern martial artists, chi is sometimes considered less mystical. It is thought of as the ability to focus. This means that using chi allows one to focus all one's energy and determination on a single goal. Because focus and single-minded determination are essential to the martial artist's best performance, the development of chi is important to the development of winning spirit.

The ability to remain calm and detached when confronted with a threat is important as well. It is considered to be an aspect of chi, so the cultivation of chi is essential to composure. A person who panics or reacts blindly to a threat will usually succumb to the threat. Fear, doubt, surprise, and confusion all adversely affect a martial artist. And all come from the martial artist's attitude. By cultivating a winning spirit, students can overcome fear, doubt, and surprise and become true martial artists.

If chi and its manifestation are relevant to your style of martial arts, be certain to teach it. Spend time meditating or practicing breathing exercises so that your students can learn to understand and successfully use chi.

4
SELF-DEFENSE TECHNIQUES
FOR WOMEN

Many women begin taking martial arts classes because they wish to learn self-defense. Almost every style of martial art has a set of self-defense techniques used to protect oneself from an attacker. These techniques may differ from those used in other aspects of martial arts training. In sparring practice, for example, partners may not be allowed to strike below the belt or to the face. But during self-defense practice, they are allowed—and even taught—to do so.

However, most martial arts base their self-defense techniques on what works for men defending themselves against other men of similar builds. Women often cannot use these techniques successfully, because their attackers will most likely be bigger and stronger than they are. When teaching self-defense techniques, this size disparity should be taken into consideration.

Practicing Self-Defense Techniques in the Training Hall

Countless times, I've seen instructors pair women with other women or even with children when teaching and practicing self-defense techniques. This is not beneficial to the students. At the minimum, you must rotate students so that each is paired with different partners of different shapes and sizes and of both genders. Working with men encourages women to develop sets of martial art techniques that work for them against any opponent (Figure 4–1). A woman might be able to defend herself against another woman with certain techniques, but those same techniques may not be adequate to defend herself against a bigger and stronger man. The only way to ascertain whether she has the skills to defend herself against a man is to partner a female martial artist with male students.

Figure 4-1

Pair female students with male students when practicing self-defense techniques.

Short women have trouble with certain self-defense techniques that require them to grab or strike the throat, nose, or eyes (Figure 4–2). It is essential for them to realize this and to learn what

a

b

Figure 4-2
Throat strikes and throat grabs may not work well for shorter women.

techniques will work better for them. You can teach your female students how to adapt different self-defense techniques (Figure 4–3). For example, suppose that you teach a defense against a chokehold that requires the martial artist to reach up and back to grab the attacker's hair. A short woman could not do this on a tall man. But she could adapt the technique and grab the attacker's shoulder, arm, or sleeve. Be willing to work with your female students to modify the self-defense tactics that you teach.

Figure 4-3
Teach your students to adapt self-defense techniques.

Physical Contact

During self-defense training, women will have to have physical contact with others. They may have to hit another person, throw another person, or perform another violent act. This can be frightening to them. In the same way, it can be frightening to be hit, to be thrown, or to have some violent act committed against you. These fears should be addressed immediately. If any of your students seem hesitant or lack confidence when practicing self-defense techniques, it may be because they are afraid. One of the ways fear can be addressed is through controlled partner work.

Controlled Partner Work

Controlled partner work merely means starting at a very basic, gentle level. Until your students become accustomed to physical contact, keep it limited and light. Have students perform their techniques without touching each other, if this is feasible (Figure 4–4).

Figure 4-4

Have students first practice their techniques without touching their partners.

Have them then move on to light touching (Figure 4–5). If you are teaching throws, have the partners work on the entry techniques and the breaking balance techniques without actually throwing. Over time students can increase their physical contact, but they should continue to do the techniques slowly and carefully (Figure 4–6). Have them add speed only after they are comfortable with physical contact. Speed adds power and increases the likelihood that mistakes will prove painful.

Women's Need to Defend Themselves

Another very important consideration to remember when teaching self-defense techniques to women is this fact: women being beaten by men is the number one reason for emergency room visits.

Figure 4-5

Have students practice their techniques using light contact.

a

Figure 4-6
Keep self-defense
techniques simple
and direct.

b

Equally disturbing is the fact that more than one in three women have been assaulted, molested, or raped. In all likelihood, some of your female students have been physically abused.

For these reasons, physical contact can be terrifying for women. But these are also the reasons women want to learn to protect themselves. This is why contact should be controlled—light and gentle—at first. Also, it is important to keep all physical contact—including any touching or physical correction you do while teaching—at a professional, neutral level.

Self-Defense and Assertiveness

You can also stress assertiveness. Often, women are discouraged from following their instincts and standing up for themselves. You can teach female students to be more assertive simply by encouraging them to use their own voices. This can be done by using a shout or kiai. Encourage women to develop a strong, solid shout. Encourage them to shout during self-defense training, just as they shout in class when performing techniques. Also, encourage them to turn the shout into a "No!" when they practice self-defense techniques. At first, your students may feel self-conscious, but time and practice will increase their comfort with shouting and it will actually make them feel more confident.

By encouraging assertiveness, you'll also make it easier for students to stand up for themselves and perhaps avoid a violent situation before it gets started. A woman who feels confident and assertive is far less likely to tolerate abuse of any kind or associate with people who would hurt her.

Self-Defense Outside the Training Hall

Self-Defense Through Awareness

In addition to teaching self-defense techniques, it is important to teach women that self-defense doesn't necessarily mean striking someone. For example, you should stress awareness of one's surroundings. When they perceive threats before they materialize, women can conduct their lives more safely.

This doesn't mean that women should live their lives behind locked and bolted doors, or that they should depend on such ruses as having a male voice on the answering machine if they live alone. It does mean learning to observe and trusting one's instincts and reactions. As a woman leaves her office, she should look around, be aware of who is in the area, and make a note of anything unusual or out of place. If anything disturbs her, she should not be embarrassed to take action. For instance, if a man loitering in the parking lot makes her nervous, she should certainly return to the office building and ask for an escort. (The escort doesn't have to be a security guard or a bouncer—a couple of coworkers, male or female, will do.) There's nothing to be self-conscious about when taking precautions—even if the man loitering in the parking lot happens to be the president of the company. The world is a dangerous place and there is nothing wrong with treating it that way.

Self-defense depends upon an awareness of your environment. Have students practice observation throughout the day. When they are in a building, have them locate the exits. Have them consider where the halls and roads lead to. Tell them to describe one or two things that they weren't aware of before this exercise, such as a door leading to the outside that they hadn't realized existed.

Practice observation in class by having one student sit with her eyes closed while several other students stand in different parts of the training hall, carrying different objects or doing different activities. Allow the student a few seconds to look around the room, then have her close her eyes again. Ask her to describe where the other students were in the room, what they were doing, and what they were carrying. This exercise, while honing observation and self-defense skills, is actually a lot of fun. Let all of your students take turns being the observer and repeat the exercise now and then.

Self-Defense and Lifestyle

An essential part of self-defense practice should be a consideration of your individual lifestyle. Ask your students to think about how they spend their time. Do they work in an office and wear a skirt and heels? If they wear skirts, they may need to practice different self-defense techniques than if they wear jeans all the time. If they usually wear tennis shoes, they can use different techniques than if they frequently wear heels. They might be able to pivot and do a sidekick wearing tennis shoes. Wearing heels, they might be able to stomp on an instep to inflict damage. A woman doesn't need to change her job or the way she dresses; she just needs to adapt her self-defense techniques to her lifestyle.

Encourage your students to practice their techniques in the clothing that they wear most frequently. This helps them see what self-defense techniques are the most useful for them.

Have students think about other aspects of their lifestyles. Do they often take the kids along with them? Do they often travel by themselves? Have your students consider their habits. If they drive a lot, they should know how to change a tire. If they visit a lot of different places in the course of a day, they should have a plan for letting someone know if they're in trouble.

Have your students consider and practice in the different terrain they visit during the course of a day (Figure 4–7). Teaching outdoors can be a lot of fun and can also demonstrate how kicking while on pavement is a different proposition altogether from kicking in the carpeted training hall. Have them practice in places similar to where

a

b

Figure 4-7
Have your students act out different self-defense scenarios.

they find themselves in the course of a day. Perhaps they spend time on a slick tile floor, or outside on hilly ground, or in a car. (Yes, even a car is a terrain.) Ask your students to consider what they would do if they were at a red light and someone attempted a carjacking. What techniques can be done when you're held in place by your seat belt? It is also important to practice self-defense techniques from the ground (Figure 4–8). Women are often thrown or fall to the ground during a violent confrontation. It is one of the most vulnerable positions to be in when defending against an attacker.

Your students should also be aware that people can do techniques much better after they have warmed up and stretched. They shouldn't count on being able to kick someone in the head if they're attacked after sitting in the movie theater for two hours. Have them visualize the situations in which they must respond to an attack and adapt their self-defense ideas to their available skills.

Figure 4-8
Teach self-defense techniques from the ground.

Further, have your students think about the advice they've been given in the past. For example, one common technique described in women's magazines is to jab your keys into the attacker's eyes. I have never really been able to imagine myself doing this to somebody. But I can visualize myself punching someone in the nose or in the Adam's apple. By visualizing themselves using different self-defense techniques, your students will be able to decide if they could actually carry them out.

Self-Defense Against a Known Assailant

It is also essential to remember that women often know their attackers. It is actually comparatively rare for a woman to be raped by a complete stranger. It is much more likely that someone she knows—an acquaintance or even a lover or a husband—will hurt her. This is another reason why it's usually not reasonable to teach a woman how to gouge someone's eyes out. If it is her husband who is hurting her, it might be very difficult for her to seriously injure him (Figure 4–9). However, she could probably throw a punch or a strike to the groin area that might stop him and enable her to get away.

Figure 4-9

A control technique stops the attack without causing permanent injury to the attacker.

As martial arts instructors, we are always teaching women what to do when complete strangers attack them, and yet this situation is not the biggest threat to women. If we arm her with mace or a handgun, is she really going to be willing to use these against her brother's best friend?

Women should visualize what self-defense techniques to use in a situation where the attacker is someone they know, such as a neighbor or their son's football coach.

Self-Defense Through Self-Esteem

The founder of aikido used to say that self-defense begins with taking care of oneself. This is a very good concept to communicate to your students, especially the women. Self-defense is often just a matter of taking care in your relationships. As we know, women are much more likely to be hurt by someone they know than by complete strangers. This is why it is important to enter into relationships cautiously and prudently. If a person seems to thrive on intimidating others, or threatens or bullies a woman, she should seriously reconsider her connection with that person.

Of course, because self-defense sometimes requires physical action, taking care of oneself is of greatest importance. This means staying in good physical condition, being alert at all times, and avoiding vulnerable situations.

Adapting Weapons for Self-Defense

If your martial arts style teaches the use of weapons, such as with certain kinds of karate or escrima, teach your female students how to adapt those techniques to other environmental weapons. Show a woman who is good at using an escrima stick how to use a golf club in the same way. Also, discuss other environmental weapons, such as throwing a vase at an attacker, or hitting with a phone, or gouging with a letter opener. A person could use fireplace or garden tools as weapons. But it is up to you to encourage your female students to see ordinary objects as possible weapons of self-defense. And it is also up to you to teach them how to use these weapons without jeopardizing their own safety.

PRAIRIE CREEK LIBRARY DISTRICT
Dwight. Illinois

Three Levels of Conflict and Defense

Remember that the main point of self-defense is escape. Be certain your students know that nothing is more important. There is no need to retaliate against an attacker and try to hurt him if the opportunity to escape arises.

Self-defense classes usually identify three levels of conflicts and three levels of defense. Conflict at a basic level occurs when someone does something you don't want them to do. In a self-defense situation, this might be someone touching or grabbing you in an unwelcome way. The level of conflict escalates when the opponent refuses to stop whatever action is making you feel uncomfortable and threatened. The final stage of conflict occurs when the attacker's clear intention is to hurt you.

A corresponding level of defense is used against each level of conflict. The first level of defense includes techniques that are used to escape an attacker. The second level includes techniques that are used to control an attacker. The third level includes techniques that are used to counter an attacker's techniques, with the intention of hurting him. Thus, a person should react differently to different levels of violence. If a martial artist unsuccessfully tries to escape from the attacker using a level one technique, the self-defense must rise to the next level, which is control. If the control level technique fails to stop the attacker, the self-defense must rise to the highest level, which is the countering level.

For example, perhaps a person grabs your shoulder. You might be able to pull away and say something such as, "leave me alone," and escape. But perhaps the attacker is more persistent than that. Perhaps you pull away and he grabs your sleeve again. This means the conflict has gone to a higher level. This time as you pull away, you would trap and control the attacker's arm. You still haven't hurt him. The conflict is still within reasonable bounds. At this point, you may still be able to persuade the attacker to back off. However, perhaps this is not enough. Perhaps even though you have controlled the attacker's hand or arm, he decides to kick you or inflict physical harm in some other way. Now the attacker's persistence has raised the conflict another notch. At this point you must counter the attacker's techniques by performing striking or other injurious techniques of your own.

Of course no encounter is going to be entirely predictable. It won't necessarily go this smoothly through the three levels of self-defense. It might be from the start that you have to defend yourself by using countering techniques. The point is that using excessive force on a man who simply grabs your arm is asking for trouble—perhaps involving the police and the legal system. You must be able to show that you felt in immediate danger of injury.

Adapting Self-Defense Techniques

Remember as you teach self-defense techniques in your martial arts classes that not all techniques work well for women. Techniques that require them to reach or demand a lot of upper body strength may not work well for them. Remember they should practice all of their self-defense techniques on men who are bigger and heavier than they are. This helps them test and adapt self-defense techniques to their own strengths and abilities (Figure 4–10).

Figure 4-10
Have students test the effectiveness of self-defense techniques against bigger partners.

You can modify the self-defense techniques you teach by considering the size disparity that women often have with men. If a self-defense technique calls for a strike to the head or face, a short woman might not be able to perform it successfully. Is there a way to adapt the technique so that she could strike to the throat or even the solar plexus (Figure 4–11)? Or, if your female students don't feel they have enough upper body strength for throws, show them how to use pivot points to break someone's balance.

a

Figure 4-11

If a student is too short to reach over her partner's arm to escape a chokehold, have her strike the partner's ribs.

b

The following self-defense techniques work well for women. They can be adapted for any of the three levels of conflict that have been discussed. Practicing these types of techniques allows women to become more confident about facing an attack—whether they know the attacker or not, and regardless of how serious the threat is.

Defense Against a Wrist Grab (Figure 4–12). To practice, have the attacker grab the defender's wrist. The defender steps forward, placing her leg against the attacker's leg. With her free hand, she grabs the attacker's shoulder and pushes down. At the same time, she grabs and pulls on the attacker's wrist. This helps her control the attacker. The defender can add a knee strike to the solar plexus.

a

Figure 4–12
Defense Against a Wrist Grab
The student steps forward, places her leg against her partner's leg, and grabs the arm to control the partner.

b

Defense Against a Double Wrist Grab (Figure 4–13). To practice, have the attacker grab both of the defender's wrists. The defender steps toward the attacker and delivers a knee strike to the solar plexus.

a

Figure 4-13

Defense Against a Double Wrist Grab

The student steps in and delivers a knee strike to the solar plexus.

b

Defense Against a Sleeve or Lapel Grab (Figure 4–14). To practice, have the attacker grab the defender's sleeve or lapel. The defender places her opposite hand on top of the attacker's. She presses her thumb against the attacker's thumb joint and peels his hand away. As she does so, she grabs the attacker's wrist with her free hand. When the attacker releases her, she maintains her grasp on his wrist and places her elbow against his in order to control his arm.

a

figure 4-14
Defense Against a Sleeve or Lapel Grab
The student peels the partner's hand away and controls his arm by placing her elbow against his.

b

c

Defense Against a Sleeve Grab from Behind (Figure 4–15). To practice, have the attacker grab the defender's sleeve from behind, as if the defender were walking away. The defender turns toward the attacker's arm and delivers a palm strike to escape.

a

Figure 4-15

Defense Against a Sleeve Grab from Behind

The student turns and delivers a palm strike to the partner's hand.

b

Defense Against a Lapel Grab (Figure 4–16). To practice, have the attacker grab the defender's lapel with one hand. The defender should reach with both hands and pull the attacker's hand down sharply, forcing him to release her lapel. The defender can use her forearm or wrist to press against the attacker's hand to gain more leverage.

a

Figure 4-16

Defense Against a Lapel Grab

The student grabs her partner's hand and pulls down.

b

Defense Against a Lapel Grab, Taller Partner (Figure 4–17). To practice, have the attacker grab the defender's lapel. The defender places her opposite hand on top of the attacker's. She presses her thumb against the attacker's thumb joint and peels the hand away. She twists the attacker's arm to control him.

a

Figure 4-17

Defense Against a Lapel Grab,
Taller Partner

The student peels her partner's hand away and twists his arm to control him.

b

c

Defense Against a Supported Chokehold (Figure 4–18). To practice, have the attacker use a chokehold against the defender. The attacker should use his other hand to "lock" or support the hold by placing it behind the defender's neck. The defender bends at the waist, swinging her closest arm up and over the attacker's arm or shoulder. The defender pushes the attacker's head and body away. She could gouge his eyes or strike to his face if needed.

a

b

Figure 4-18

Defense Against a Supported Chokehold

The student bends at the waist, swings her arm up and behind her partner, and pushes his head away. She could gouge his eyes or strike to his face if necessary.

c

d

Defense Against a Full Nelson (Figure 4–19). To practice, have the attacker use a full nelson against the defender. The attacker should slide his arms beneath the defender's, then lock his hands behind the defender's neck. The defender simply raises her arms and slides through the attacker's hold. She could also deliver a back kick to the knee or groin in order to loosen the hold before escaping.

a

Figure 4-19

Defense Against a Full Nelson

The student raises her arms and slides through her partner's hold.

b

5

Sparring Strategies
for Women

Martial arts training usually consists of the practice of a variety of skills, including forms, the repetition of basic techniques, self-defense, and some type of freestyle sparring. From the beginning of martial arts practice, women often enjoy performing many of these different skills. Many enjoy forms, because doing forms requires grace, balance, and timing, like dancing. They understand how it enhances the art, and they realize it helps them practice their techniques in a logical way and in a constricted space. They may also like basic techniques because this practice helps them feel powerful and strong and confirms in their own minds that they are martial artists. Finally, many women are eager to work on self-defense techniques because they can directly impact their lives. The main reason that women begin martial arts practice is to learn such techniques and to develop the confidence to apply them.

Unfortunately, few women truly enjoy another important aspect of martial arts training when they are first introduced to it: sparring. Most women who dislike sparring at first eventually come to enjoy it. Still, sparring can often be the reason why women discontinue martial arts training. In addition to their fear of hitting others and being hit, few women can relate to an activity that requires such physical contact.

Customizing Sparring Practice for Women

Contact

Many schools expect little or light contact during sparring. Even schools that allow hard contact sparring should insist that contact be controlled. The point is to prevent injury and improve sparring. As the instructor, always remember to keep an eye on how much contact occurs during sparring matches between students. Be ready to make partners back down from the amount of contact they're using. This should hold true in all cases, but it is especially important when big men spar smaller women.

It takes a while for a martial arts student to understand how to spar well. Unlike other areas of martial arts practice, competence in sparring takes a long time to achieve. A beginning student can be taught basic movements or techniques and after a short period of time be able to perform them adequately. In the same way, the practice of forms is usually encouraging for students. Beginners learn beginner forms. A form may not be easy for them to perform, but most students believe they will understand and master it eventually. As a student advances in the martial arts, his or her forms become more difficult, which increases the challenge and keeps things interesting.

But none of this is true in sparring. Sparring is complicated, frustrating, and difficult to master. At many schools, a beginning student spars with different partners of different skill levels right away. The disparity in skill level can be frustrating. However, many instructors believe that it is only through sparring with partners who have superior skills that students can become proficient. Still, the period of time it takes to master even the basic techniques of sparring can be enormously discouraging for martial artists.

You can assure your martial arts students that they will eventually master the basics of sparring and encourage them to continue their practice, but some will never learn to enjoy sparring. There's not a lot you can do about this. You shouldn't stop requiring sparring just because some students don't like it. And you shouldn't make it optional. You must always expect all of your students to meet the same standards.

However, one thing you can do to help is to insist that your students spar within a few levels of their partner's abilities. Many instructors make a rule that higher ranking students can use only the lower belt techniques when sparring with lower belt students. That is, if a beginning fighter at a beginning belt level (such as a yellow belt) is taught the front kick, the reverse kick, and the sidekick, these are the only kicks that can be used by others who are sparring that student. A brown belt cannot use his or her more advanced brown belt techniques. This helps the lower belt feel more competent and less overwhelmed. Higher ranking belts should also be expected to use lighter or no contact and should try not to overwhelm the student with their skill.

Sparring Based on Male Models

Many women get frustrated with sparring because much of what they are taught is based on male models. And rightfully so: what works for a man when sparring another man does not necessarily work for women. A woman sparring a man is often at a disadvantage. Just as in self-defense training, a short woman may not be able to do certain techniques successfully when sparring a tall man. Frequently, students are taught a style of sparring that plays to men's strengths and handicaps most women.

One of the ways to help women become better at sparring is to present their size difference as an advantage instead of a drawback. Most women have less body mass than most men. For this reason they will need to rely on speed, which can actually level the sparring field. A fast woman is as powerful as a big man. You just have to convince her that this is so.

Be certain that all of your students spar both men and women. It is helpful to men because women have speed and flexibility that is difficult for men to duplicate. This allows them to learn how to counter such techniques. Women should spar men to learn how to counter mass and muscle (and only men present the opportunity for them to face a muscular 250 pounder). Do not separate your students along gender lines during martial arts practice. It is important for women to develop the confidence that comes from sparring big men and it is important for men to be exposed to the abilities of women (Figure 5–1).

a

b

Figure 5-1

Women should spar men of different sizes and skill levels.

Sparring Styles

Although each student will develop his or her own sparring style, you should be willing to help your female students customize their techniques to account for the fact that they tend to be shorter, smaller, and lighter than many of their opponents. A bigger man can deliver more powerful strikes and has a longer reach—natural advantages when it comes to sparring. But women can compensate for these advantages by careful training. They can work on flexibility to increase their range and the reach of their kicks. This neutralizes a taller person's advantages. Women can also work on developing speed, especially explosive speed, in order to counteract a big man's obvious advantages (Figure 5–2).

a

Figure 5-2

Takedowns and throws rely on speed and agility, not muscle and mass.

b

In addition, female fighters should learn specific strategies and tactics to compensate for size disadvantages. Because women have less reach with their arms and legs, they need to get in close in order to score points on their opponents. Therefore it is very important for them to learn how to fight inside: to get past the opponent's defense without being scored on. Women can rely on their flexibility and speed, which they can improve through sparring drills.

Sparring Techniques

Sparring Drills

To encourage flexibility and speed, have your students practice timing drills. Teach countering techniques and have partners work together to learn how to counter defensive tactics and move inside. The bigger partner can perform a technique while the smaller partner counters. This counter should enable her to move inside, getting past the bigger partner's defense. In a drill, for example, if one partner performs a roundhouse kick, the other partner can respond with a reverse kick followed by a punch. The reverse kick keeps the attacking partner occupied. With the punch, the defending partner has moved inside and into a range where she can perform techniques that will score points. Have students practice variations of this drill using different techniques.

Defensive Maneuvers

You should also teach your students footwork and body shifting. Because women are usually faster and more agile, they can make footwork and body shifting work to their advantage. These basic defensive maneuvers can be taught using drills in which one partner strikes using a series of different techniques while the defending partner uses body shifting or footwork to move out of the way and set up a strike of her own.

Body Movement (Body Shifting)

Body movement or body shifting means turning the upper body away or pivoting on one foot to avoid a strike. Accomplished body shifters can twist at the waist, let the punch or kick slide by, and then follow with a countering technique of their own.

Have your students practice body movement with one partner performing a technique while the other tries to shift his or her body out of the way. (Remind students not to take steps to move out of the way; they should concentrate on maneuvering their bodies.)

Footwork

Footwork can help sparring as well. Because of their speed, women are likely to benefit from training in footwork. By stepping away from a punch or a kick, the martial artist can often avoid being struck while at the same time setting up a technique to counter with. Footwork varies according to the martial arts discipline, but three simple patterns are common and can easily be taught. They are stepping left, stepping right, and triangular stepping. The first two are self-explanatory. The trick is knowing which way to step. This can be taught with drills in which one partner strikes toward the other. The other partner steps left or right to avoid the strike. Instead of physically blocking the partner's techniques, one simply steps away from them.

Triangular stepping is also just like it sounds. One simply steps in a triangle. This means stepping back, to the side, and then in; or stepping to the side, to the back, and then away. Each variation requires practice. Stepping in puts you in fighting range; stepping away gets you out of range (useful for avoiding attacks). Triangular stepping is an excellent technique to use against experienced opponents. If they anticipate your stepping left or right, they will be confused with triangular stepping. It also helps women to avoid their opponents' techniques by putting themselves inside quickly.

Practice this using drills. For example, if her partner does a front kick, a student can move out of the way using a triangular step. This allows her to be in range to punch to her partner's ribs, while avoiding being struck herself. Footwork and body shifting also prevent the partner with a size advantage from landing a lot of points.

Kicking Techniques

One of the most productive things a female martial artist can do is to develop a strong arsenal of kicks. Most martial artists rely on just a few kicks, particularly in sparring. Many sparring martial artists use only a roundhouse kick, a sidekick, and a reverse kick. This is a weakness that can be exploited by teaching your students how to master counters for these techniques—such as a reverse kick and a punch to counter a roundhouse kick or a reverse kick. Since these few kicks are so heavily relied upon, a good counterattack can easily succeed.

But because women have speed, flexibility, and agility, they should master a number of kicks in their sparring. Then they will be less likely to find their kicking weaknesses exploited.

Teach them the crescent kick, the reverse crescent kick, and the hooking kick. Show your female students how to add these to their sparring. Also teach them how to do double kicks—performing two kicks in a row without setting the foot down. One kick may be to the middle section to lower the partner's guard, with the next kick going to the high section. Have partners work together in drills, with one doing a specific technique such as a roundhouse kick, while the other responds with a less common kick or a double kick. As students practice, have them go faster until they match their sparring speed.

By focusing on teaching ways to penetrate a defense, countering common techniques, using defensive maneuvers, and diversifying kicks, you can help your female students become proficient—even excellent—fighters.

6
Mastering Martial Arts Techniques Designed for Men

Every single martial arts technique can be mastered by women. Some techniques just require more patience and training for women. On the other hand, women usually master techniques that require speed or flexibility more easily than men.

Why Techniques Can Be Difficult to Master

The techniques of most martial arts were created by men for men. The main reason women may have difficulty with these techniques is that they are built differently. A less obvious reason is that women tend to be less attuned to their own bodies and their abilities. Women usually need some time and effort to become familiar with how their bodies work. Meanwhile, you can offer some suggestions to help women master the techniques that tend to be more difficult for them.

Mastering Lower Body Techniques

Jumping Kicks

One example of a technique that gives women trouble is the jumping kick. Such kicks can play an important part in some martial arts.

Therefore, it is important for women to master jumping kicks instead of being allowed to perform them less than adequately. Of course, many women perform high jumping kicks perfectly. But plenty of women have difficulty with them. The first problem, of course, is that women have a lower center of gravity than men. Because much of their weight rests in their hips and thighs, it is more difficult for them to get a lot of height on the jumps. Also, they may not have developed the explosive power in their legs that is necessary for truly excellent jumping kicks.

To help overcome these problems, teach your students to improve their jumping techniques by separating each technique into its various parts. A front jump kick can be broken into the jump and the front kick itself. Have your students first practice jumping without worrying about the kick. Challenge them to jump as high as they can and still maintain their balance both as they rise and as they land. Once they are able to do this, they should work on the kick, learning to chamber it tightly and strike with the kick correctly. Then have them put the jump and the kick together.

Since each jumping technique requires a slightly different kind of jump, each jump should be practiced separately. For a jump reverse kick, the martial artist must rotate while in the air. This is much different than a jump front kick, where the martial artist faces the target when he or she jumps and then strikes it directly. To teach your students to jump for the jump reverse kick, have them jump and tuck their legs under so that their calves touch their thighs. This helps them gain more height in their kicks but also puts their legs in a better position to perform the kicking technique. Once they're proficient with the jumping and tucking, have them work separately on the kick, chambering tightly and turning quickly to the target. Finally, have them combine the kick and the jump.

Plyometric Drills

To improve explosive muscle strength necessary for jumping techniques, include plyometric drills in your classes. Such drills improve the martial artist's ability to perform jumping kicks, but they also build muscle strength and sharpen reflexes.

Start with a simple jumping drill. Stack some kicking targets on the floor. (If you don't have kicking targets, use cushions or pillows.) Have students jump from one side of the stack to the other as quickly as possible without pausing between jumps. Their goal should be to go as fast as they can without knocking the targets over. Stack the targets higher to challenge students as they become more proficient.

A sweeping drill requires students to work in pairs. One partner should use a target or focus mitt and sweep at the other partner's feet. The other partner must jump up to avoid being struck. Partners should work quickly and not allow pauses between jumps.

Another favorite plyometric drill is the frog jump (Figure 6–1). Have students crouch on the floor and jump as high into the air as possible. They should land in their original crouching position. Do frog jumps up and down the training hall for a few minutes after each class. This is a very tiring exercise, but it will help your students develop explosive power quickly.

Mastering Upper Body Techniques

Because most women have much stronger lower bodies, they will tend to use leg and kicking techniques. While this is a very good idea because it allows them to use their strength to their advantage, they should also be encouraged to improve their upper body power. Many martial arts, such as aikido and judo, require considerable upper body strength to achieve expertise. But regardless of which martial arts they participate in, women will improve their performance by increasing their upper body strength.

In addition to improving strength through weight training and other muscle building exercises, your female students can be taught to add power to their hand techniques simply by using the power of their entire body. One of the most common mistakes martial artists make is to use only their arms to generate power when they strike with hand techniques. For example, a martial artist will throw a punch from the shoulder. The only power behind such a punch is the power of the arm. If your arm isn't very strong, your punch won't be very strong, either. But immediate, dramatic improvements can be made by using the hips as a pivot point to throw the whole body into the strike.

Figure 6-1

Frog jumps are done by crouching and jumping into the air, then landing in the crouched position.

a

b

c

Generating Power

To teach the use of the entire body to generate power, have students assume a front stance position. They should chamber their fists near their waists. As they punch forward, have them twist the same side hip forward as well. (Remind them not to reach or overextend their arms.) If they are punching a target or a heavy bag, they should notice a difference immediately. You can also have them step into a punch to add body power behind the hand technique. Stepping or sliding as well as turning or pivoting the hips creates very powerful hand techniques.

Have your students practice how these different strategies feel by using the heavy bag or kicking targets. Have them punch the bag using just the arm from the shoulder down. Then have them pivot their hips into the punch. Next have them step or slide into the punch. They should notice immediate differences in power. To generate the most power, they should combine the hip pivot with the slide or step. To get the most from these tips, students should practice punching the heavy bag a few minutes each day. Don't limit this exercise to the punch: have them practice using their body weight with other hand techniques as well. If no heavy bag is available, have them use a makiwara board (a striking post) or a similar target.

Boxing Techniques

To help your students improve their upper body strength, you can also teach them the basics of boxing. Boxing the heavy bag certainly builds upper body strength, can be an enjoyable alternative to lifting weights, and offers students the opportunity to learn a few useful techniques.

Most martial arts do not teach jabs, crosses, hooks, and upper cuts—but that doesn't mean they aren't effective techniques for your students to learn anyway. Helping your students to understand the techniques of boxing will help them improve their upper body strength and can increase the power of their hand techniques.

Building Upper Body Strength

Upper body strength can also be achieved by using old-fashioned exercises. Push-ups are an excellent way to strengthen the upper arms and chest muscles. If students cannot perform push-ups very easily, have them begin with their knees on the floor. Have them do as many push-ups as they can at one time. As they improve, raise the difficulty by having them rest only their toes on the floor. Once they master this, they can move on to the old martial arts standby: the knuckle push-up. This helps them strengthen their wrists and their hands in order to improve their punching and hand-striking techniques.

You can also encourage your female students to do some weight training to improve their upper body strength. They can practice basic weight training at home with inexpensive free weights. Simple biceps curls and triceps extensions are excellent ways to build upper body strength.

Confidence

Of course, the key to mastering any technique is to work with confidence. Teach your students to commit themselves to every technique they use. If they're tentative or unsure about their techniques, they will never be very powerful. To overcome their hesitancy, have your students work on confidence-building drills.

Have one partner stand still while the other partner strikes. The striking partner should perform one technique, such as a punch, repeatedly. The striking partner should practice working as fast, as powerfully, and as confidently as possible. The striking partner should strike toward the defending partner without making contact. As your students gain confidence, they can work toward light contact with the uniform (or workout clothing). As they grow more skilled, they can start to touch the partner. This not only gives them confidence in their techniques, it helps them to understand and use control so that they do not injure their partners.

Women sometimes get frustrated with the emphasis on upper body techniques (and in some martial arts, the jumping techniques). But women can master all these techniques with time, effort, and guidance.

Natural Advantages

Keep in mind that women have certain characteristics that give them a definite advantage in the martial arts: superior flexibility, greater agility, and strong kicking. Teach your female students how to use their assets. Emphasizing these strengths quickly improves the martial arts performance of most women.

The Flexibility Advantage

Women are naturally more flexible than men, so they enjoy distinct advantages in almost any martial art. This can help them stay motivated because they achieve improvement more quickly than men. Women are also able to attain greater flexibility overall than their male counterparts.

For female martial artists, flexibility can be used to overcome disadvantages. If most of her partners are taller, they have longer legs and can reach farther. But a woman can neutralize this advantage because her flexibility enables her to kick higher than her male partner. Flexibility also increases the fighting range. Finally, the flexible female martial artist has a greater range of techniques at her disposal. For example, the crescent or ax kick requires flexibility in the hip and the hamstring area, which prevents many men from kicking as high as the shoulder or head. Women, however, can use this technique to the greatest effect. Identify what specific techniques in your martial arts style require the most flexibility, and encourage your female students to practice them.

Flexibility is also essential in martial arts such as aikido, judo, and jujutsu. It allows for easier grappling and also makes women harder to pin. Joint locks are less effective on a flexible woman, and she can more easily counter them.

The Speed Advantage

The most important mathematical formula for a martial artist to remember is mass times speed equals power. This means that a bigger person is not necessarily more powerful than a smaller person. Because women are usually lighter and less muscular than men, they are generally quicker—and this speed translates into power. For this reason, women can be just as powerful as men.

Women can use speed techniques in favor of muscle or mass techniques. For example, a spinning wheel kick is a speed technique. It requires speed alone to be effective. If you do not perform it quickly enough, the technique will not work regardless of how much muscle you have behind it. On the other hand, a sidekick is a mass or muscle technique. If you are slow and have a big body, the technique can still be very powerful. Of course a speed technique such as the spinning wheel kick benefits from added strength, while a mass or muscle technique such as the sidekick can be improved with the addition of speed.

Speed techniques are excellent for women to use. Spinning techniques and whipping techniques, such as the roundhouse kick, make excellent choices for women. In addition, because of their speed, women can often perform complicated combinations of kicks more effectively than men. For instance, the double kick, which is performed by striking twice with the leg without setting it down between strikes, is a kicking combination that requires speed to be effective. These and other combinations can be performed very well by women.

Teaching Speed

One way to teach your female students to capitalize on their potential speed is through relaxation. Remind them that when their muscles are tight and tense, their techniques will be slower. Often, martial artists clench their muscles to generate power, but this actually slows the technique and reduces its power. Therefore, remind your students that they should relax their muscles as they practice their techniques to increase their speed.

The clench-and-release exercise helps students to learn how a relaxed muscle feels. Tell your students to tighten the muscles in their arm as much as possible, and then completely relax them. Remind your students that a more relaxed muscle moves more swiftly toward the target.

To convince your students that relaxation leads to speed, have them tighten the muscles in their arm and then punch a heavy bag. Then have them relax the muscles in their arm and punch the heavy bag again. They will see that the relaxed arm moves to the target faster.

Of course, a completely relaxed hand or foot doesn't strike with the same amount of impact as one in which the muscles are tightened. The hand or foot might flop, twist, or bend. Therefore, to increase the power of the impact, the muscle should be tightened just as the technique lands. This allows the strike to land solidly and swiftly.

Explaining these strategies to your female students will enable them to master any martial arts technique that they are taught. Although you should encourage them to take advantage of their speed, flexibility, and strong lower bodies, they also need to develop the strength and abilities to successfully perform every technique that you teach.

7

Competition Strategies and Tactics for Women

One of the surprising pleasures of the martial arts is participating in competition. Some people are competitors from the beginning and thrive on the many opportunities for competition available in martial arts. These may be informal competitions encountered in daily class. Sometimes the competition is internal. Sometimes the competition of having others watch us and evaluate us spurs us to practice more methodically. But formal competition in the martial arts, such as participating in a martial arts tournament, is a challenging and rewarding activity regardless of whether we win or lose.

Benefits of Competition

But many women don't believe this. Many women have never had the chance to compete in sporting events. Although some women deeply dislike competition against others, it can be a good way to learn how to react to a difficult situation. Competing in a tournament is stressful. It helps you see how you would perform if you were called upon to use your martial arts techniques in an unpleasant situation. But because you test yourself under controlled conditions, it's a safe stress.

Of course, we also sometimes wonder how accomplished we really are as martial artists. Entering a competition allows us to judge this. It also allows us to compete against and watch people other than our classmates.

Of course, some forms of martial arts, such as traditional aikido, do not encourage competition. Such schools feel that competition contradicts the purpose of martial arts: personal growth and self-knowledge. But most martial arts do encourage competition, at least on an occasional basis.

But women do not necessarily like competition and often have to be encouraged and taught how to participate. Remind them that the point of competition is not winning or losing—the experience is valuable in and of itself. One of the ways you can make competition more appealing to your female students is to make the preparation for competition a cooperative endeavor that stresses learning and improving over winning and losing. This emphasizes the benefits of competition while minimizing some of its drawbacks.

Preparing for Competition

For many women, practicing for tournaments requires special attention. Because many have doubts about their ability to compete, they need to bolster their confidence ahead of time. Repeated practice will help increase their confidence. Remind them that their first competition may make them so nervous they fail—and that's okay. If possible, steer them to competitions that you are familiar with. You might also sponsor your own competitions—even in-school competitions—so that your students, especially the beginners, can compete against their peers in comfortable, safe surroundings. Once they are more comfortable with the idea of formal competition, they can be encouraged to seek out other opportunities.

Practice Tournament Conditions

Lack of experience or preparation can lead to frustrating, disappointing experiences. For this reason, make certain your students have as much information as possible about the tournament or competition beforehand. They should know the rules and should be prepared for unexpected developments. Students should prepare by practicing the techniques they'll be using during the competition. In addition to allowing them extra time for practicing their form or their sparring, try to reproduce tournament conditions during practice. For example, when they practice their form, have several students watch and act as a panel of judges, just like the student will encounter during competition. Ask the student-judges to help the performing student improve her form.

Set up a sparring ring, complete with corner judges, center ring judge (referee), and scorekeeper. Have students practice sparring according to the rules of the tournament. One thing that often surprises sparring students is that some tournaments stop the action to award points. If one fighter scores a point, the referee has the pair stop sparring, moves them back to their marks, and asks for the judges to award a point. Then the match resumes. Students who are used to continuous sparring—especially those who rely on countering techniques—may find this frustrating and confusing. They may score fewer points and have to adjust the way they spar. Practice tournament sparring by the point system to help your students become accustomed to it.

Also, have your students rehearse any introductions they have to make. In many tournaments, competitors must introduce themselves to the judges and announce what they are planning to do (a certain form, a specific board break). Even this part of competition can be nerve-racking if it isn't practiced ahead of time.

Choose the Best Tournament

Guide your students in choosing tournaments to compete in. Tournaments vary widely in how they are conducted. Some are invitation-only; some are open to anyone in a clean uniform. It is usually best for women to start at invitational tournaments with which you are familiar or have previously participated in.

Regional or local tournaments make a good starting point for students new to competition. New martial artists should avoid national and international tournaments until they've gained some tournament experience. But if no regional or local invitational tournaments are available, and you aren't interested in hosting an in-school competition, by all means encourage your students to participate in a national tournament just for the experience, realizing they probably won't win on the first try.

A variety of tournaments are offered. Single-style tournaments focus on only one martial art, such as karate or tae kwon do. Open-style or multiple-style tournaments include a variety of styles. Beginning students should probably stick with the smaller single-style tournaments at first, because they will seem more familiar, and it's usually easier to compete against people who are using similar techniques.

Anticipate Tournament Divisions

In single-style tournaments, divisions are usually simple and straightforward. Events are categorized under adults' and children's divisions; adult groups usually have separate men's and women's divisions. Frequently an executive division exists for participants who are thirty-five and older.

The majority of competitors at any tournament are male. The men's competition can have several divisions at each belt level. For example, in forms competition at the black belt level, there may be age divisions, weight divisions, or degree divisions (or sometimes a combination of these). One division may include men aged eighteen to twenty-one, while men aged twenty-two to twenty-five compete in another. Or there may be a lightweight division, a medium-weight division, and a heavyweight division. Or first-degree black belts will compete in a different division from second-degree black belts, and third-degree black belts will compete in a different division from fourth-degree black belts.

Such divisions are very rarely the case in women's competition. The smaller, single-style competitions in particular have very few female competitors, so they are usually grouped into fewer divisions. For example, it is not uncommon for women to compete in a single black belt division, comprising black belts of all ages, sizes, and degree levels. This means younger women compete with older women, and taller people spar shorter competitors. To some degree, this makes the women's competition much more difficult, and students should prepare for this when practicing for their events. Women should also approach the competition with an open mind. Tournament directors sometimes have adult women compete with adult men when there are not enough women to form a competitive division.

It is also important to realize that below the black belt level, female color belts are often grouped together in a single division. As a brown belt, I once sparred a yellow belt in competition. In tae kwon do, this means that a person who was nearly a black belt was sparring someone who was just promoted from white belt. Although my opponent was given points to start, the matchup seemed very unequal and unfair. It was very difficult for me to compete appropriately. If I had been better prepared for this possibility, I might have been able to develop the right frame of mind. Women of unequal skill level competing against one another is not uncommon in tournaments. This is another reason to encourage more of your female students to compete in tournaments—so that the divisions can become larger and divided more fairly.

Explain the Rules

Make certain that your students understand the rules of the tournament ahead of time. For example, in sparring competition participants may be required to wear protective gear. If students are not accustomed to sparring in gear, they will be at a disadvantage. In the same way, if the tournament competitors don't wear gear, encourage your students to practice without it (with good control!) so that they can get used to how it feels.

Some tournaments may not allow hand techniques or kicks to the head. Students should prepare for such tournaments by refraining from these techniques when sparring in class.

Be certain students understand about fouls and disqualifications. Remind them that stepping out of the ring on purpose or turning their back on a competitor is grounds for disqualification or at least for a point deduction. Clarify with students any rules the tournament director has decided to enforce. These can be established by obtaining a tournament program or by talking with its director.

Strategies and Tactics

Once students are aware of the tournament rules, they can begin devising strategies and tactics. Although the experience of competing is more important than whether one wins or loses, most instructors prefer to help their students win at competitions. Certain strategies and tactics can be especially helpful for women competitors. These strategies and tactics vary, depending on what area of the martial arts a woman competes in—sparring, forms, or board-breaking competition.

First, overall attitude is important. A confident woman is more likely to do well. Beyond that, base your strategies on common sense. Because women's divisions are so fluid, women martial artists should develop their confidence by practicing with partners of all ranks, shapes, and sizes. And, as stated previously, practice should follow the tournament rules and simulate its environment as much as possible.

Sparring Competition

For sparring competition, playing smart is always a better idea than trying to showcase all your fancy techniques. Competitors shouldn't make big changes in their sparring style before competition—just enough to conform to tournament rules, if necessary. But beyond that, it is important to spar with confidence. Because a two-minute round can go quickly, a competitor should not spend too much time feeling out the opponent. Competitors should incorporate feints and counters in their attacks instead of spending valuable moments circling or jabbing.

Don't assume that if your female students have been practicing with men that they'll find sparring women easy. Women are faster and more flexible than men. Also, some of the techniques that work against men won't work against other women. For instance, a woman may successfully use spinning techniques against slower, bigger men. These may not work so well against women. If a student's sparring style is to try to go inside, don't be surprised if her opponents share this goal.

Keep in mind that women competing will spar others who are closer to them in height, so if your student is in kicking range, then her opponent is in kicking range; if your student is in punching range, so is her opponent. This requires a slightly different strategy than when women spar men. Spend time drilling in blocking and countering techniques so that your female students are prepared. Also, since the fighting range among women usually doesn't vary as widely as it does between women and men, they spar together more continuously instead of ducking into and out of range. Have students practice combination drills to prepare them for this. Pair up students and have them assume fighting stances. One student should "attack" the other with a variety of techniques, one after the other. The "defender" simply steps away from the attack without trying to defend. After the attacking partner has performed six or eight techniques, the other partner should be allowed to attack.

Forms Competition

In forms competition, grace, definition of techniques, agility, balance, flexibility, and coordination are all admired. Women have these qualities in spades. But two flaws frequently plague women's form competition. One is performing the form too slowly, which can make it seem less graceful. Some judges may wonder if the competitor has really learned the form or if she has forgotten what comes next. The other problem is lack of power. Although women can make their forms look artful, judges often want to see forms done with power. They are, after all, martial arts techniques. A good rule of thumb is to do the techniques swiftly, but one at a time (to define them). Make the techniques fast and solid. Slow down slightly between the techniques to add power and snap to the form.

Women can also build power into their forms by practicing with a partner holding a target. As the woman performs each technique, she should concentrate on striking the target with power. The partner can also help her stay strong and solid by having her stop at various points in the form; the partner should then try to push her off-balance. Women who attempt to perform powerfully sometimes bounce off the ground as a result. Have students stay solid and low to avoid this. (They can imagine they're in a room with a low ceiling.) Also, videotape their practices to help them see what they're doing. This is especially helpful with women who feel alienated from their bodies.

Breaking Competition

In breaking competitions (which are limited mostly to tae kwon do and a few karate schools), the main goal for women is to break all the boards. In men's competition, breaking all the boards simply keeps you in the running. To impress judges, a male competitor must perform flashy or very powerful techniques in addition to breaking all the boards. In women's competition, however, breaking all the boards is often enough for a win. In fact, a female breaking competitor once finished in third place without breaking a single board. Therefore, your female students should be reminded to use techniques that break the boards. Even simple techniques, such as a sidekick or a palm strike, that break the boards on the first try will put a woman at a much better advantage than more difficult techniques that do not consistently break the boards.

Also, moving smoothly through a sequence of breaks is admired. Competitors shouldn't stop at each board while working up the confidence to break it. Practicing board breaks is essential, as is approaching this aspect of the competition with confidence and self-assurance.

Judges tend to be male and, as such, they often look for power techniques in breaking competition and are impressed when women use them. A jump reverse kick through two boards will usually win over a spinning wheel kick through one board and an axe kick through a second, even though those kicks require excellent speed and technique.

By being aware of some of the differences between men's and women's competition, you will be able to guide your female students through competition more effectively. Understanding why they might be reluctant to compete and bolstering their self-confidence through practice can produce excellent competitors— or at least students who find the competition itself rewarding.

8
Injury Prevention

Many women who begin training in the martial arts have little sports experience. Because the martial arts seem to offer more than just a workout, women who don't consider themselves athletic will often join a school. And it is true that the martial arts are not just about physical fitness. But because of this mindset, we sometimes overlook the amount of stress that martial arts practice can actually place on our bodies. All martial arts students—especially those who lack athletic experience—must be careful to avoid getting injured. Fortunately, most martial arts injuries—the most common of which are overuse injuries, sprains, and strains—can be prevented.

Because women are frequently enthusiastic when they begin training in the martial arts, they approach everything with lots of energy. This can make them susceptible to injury. Remind your students, especially those who are not particularly fit, to start slowly and to build up their level of exercise. This will help them prevent beginner injuries.

Most martial artists talk about injuries as if they were inevitable. However, following sensible precautions can prevent many common injuries. Warming up, stretching, and cooling down after a workout are essential to avoiding injuries.

Common Injuries

Women are prone to certain injuries more frequently than men. Because women have a different weight distribution than men, they more frequently injure their hips. Because women use their legs more, they incur more leg injuries—especially knee problems. Your awareness of these tendencies can help your female students avoid injury.

Overuse Injuries

Overuse injuries like tendinitis and bursitis occur when a joint is used repeatedly—especially when the joint has not been used in that way before. These injuries often occur when beginners train too enthusiastically. Their bodies simply are not prepared for this stress. Overuse injuries also occur among those who are training heavily for competition or rank promotion testing.

To prevent the pain and discomfort of overuse injuries, be certain that students stretch before training. You can also teach your students appropriate stretching exercises during class.

To avoid overuse injuries (as well as strains and sprains), martial artists also must execute techniques precisely. If students don't pivot correctly when they kick, for instance, they are likely to put extra stress on their knees and hips, which can cause many problems.

Acute Injuries

While overuse injuries are associated with excessive use of the joint over the course of time, strains, sprains, tears, cuts, and bruises are all usually the result of acute injury—that is, a single event causes the injury. Sprains and strains can range from mild to severe, with the more serious requiring a break from training.

Muscle cramps, although not exactly an injury, cause pain and discomfort for martial artists. Sudden sharp pain or lumps of muscle tissue that can be seen or felt signal a muscle cramp. These happen when muscles are injured or overused. Fatigue and dehydration can worsen cramps. Muscle cramps usually subside without special treatment, unless they are caused by an underlying muscle injury.

Fractures, while not common, sometimes occur during martial arts training. A fracture is not always obvious. Pain, loss of function, swelling, and change in the look of a bone all indicate the possibility of fracture. Some fractures, such as stress fractures, occur over time. They are like overuse injuries. The rcpeated blows a bone takes sometimes causes a break or a series of small cracks that have the same effect as a fracture. Stress fractures (usually of the hand or the foot) are the most common fractures to occur in martial arts training.

Dislocation—when bones are pulled out of place in the joint—sometimes occurs after an acute injury. Dislocations are more likely to occur with throwing techniques. All fractures and dislocations require immediate medical attention.

Prevention and Treatment

Most injuries can be prevented by using common sense. Be certain each class has a warming up, stretching, and cooling down period (Figure 8–1). Also encourage your students to warm up and stretch before class and on their own to prevent muscles from being injured while cold.

Figure 8-1
Remind students to stretch and cool down after class.

PRAIRIE CREEK LIBRARY DISTRICT
Dwight. Illinois

Warm-ups help to avoid injury but also significantly reduce muscle stiffness and soreness. Stretching also helps increase flexibility. Certain stretches can be especially helpful to prevent those injuries to which more women are prone.

To help prevent acute injury, encourage the use of protective padding such as sparring gear. This is especially helpful for beginners, who may not know their own power or who may make mistakes that lead to sparring injuries. Have students use bag gloves or sparring gloves when they are punching a bag or a striking post, at least until they feel very competent. Also insist that students do not wear jewelry in class because of the potential injury to partners.

You should have at least a basic knowledge of first aid as an instructor. Many schools require every teacher to be certified in CPR and first aid. This is a very good idea. Training sessions can even be sponsored at your school by a local hospital or the Red Cross—often at little or no cost to you. This is a convenient way for you and your students to earn certification. Keep a first aid kit on hand to treat any minor injuries that crop up.

Stretching

You can teach your students stretches and you can incorporate them into your classes to reduce the likelihood of injury (Figure 8–2). The following stretches are designed to help women prevent common martial arts injuries.

Figure 8-2

Incorporate stretching as a part of class to help avoid injuries.

Stance Stretches. Stance stretches are based on the stances in which martial artists perform their techniques. The most common of these are the horse stance stretch and the back stance (or fighting stance) stretch. Of course, any stance may be used. The martial artist assumes the stance and then lowers it by bending her knees deeply. Some martial artists use stance stretches to build strength by holding the stretch for several minutes at a time. Stance stretches should be avoided by martial artists with knee problems.

Horse Stance Stretch (Figure 8–3). Assume a solid horse stance position, feet about a shoulder and a half's width apart, feet facing forward, kees bent. From this position, bend the knees and lower the stance until the stretch is felt on the tops of the thighs. Hold the stretch for ten seconds, then relax and repeat.

Figure 8-3
Horse Stance Stretch
The student assumes a horse stance position, then lowers the stance until she feels the stretch.

Back Stance Stretch (Figure 8–4). Assume a solid back stance (or fighting stance) position, feet perpendicular to each other, weight resting primarily on the back leg. From this position, bend the knees and lower the stance until the stretch is felt. Hold the stretch for ten seconds, then relax and repeat. Switch legs so that the forward foot alternates.

Figure 8-4

Back Stance Stretch

The student assumes a back stance position, then lowers the stance until she feels the stretch.

Groin and Hamstring Stretch (Figure 8–5). Sit on the floor, tucking one leg in. The other leg extends straight out. Then bend forward, reaching toward the toes, trying to touch the foot with both hands. When a full stretch is reached, hold the position for fifteen seconds, then relax and repeat. Switch legs so that the extended leg alternates.

Figure 8-5

Groin and Hamstring Stretch

The student sits on the floor and tucks one leg in. She extends the other leg and reaches for her toes. She holds the stretch for fifteen seconds and repeats it using the other leg.

Hip Stretch (Figure 8–6). Sit on the floor, extending both legs. Bring one knee to the chest, using hands if necessary. Hold the position for fifteen seconds, then relax and repeat. Switch legs.

Figure 8-6

Hip Stretch

The student extends both legs and then brings one knee to her chest. She holds the stretch for fifteen seconds and repeats it using the other leg.

Hip and Groin Stretch (Figure 8–7). Sit on the floor and slide both feet in until the soles are touching and the knees are bent out to the side. Bend forward toward the floor. Hold the stretch for fifteen seconds, then relax and repeat.

Figure 8-7
Hip and Groin Stretch
The student sits on the floor, pulls both legs in, then bends toward the floor (holding the stretch for fifteen seconds).

Hip Flexor Stretch (Figure 8–8). Kneel with one knee and foot flat on the floor. The other knee should be bent at a ninety-degree angle. Rock forward gently until you feel the stretch on the top of your hip. Hold the stretch for fifteen seconds, then relax and repeat with the other leg.

Figure 8-8

Hip Flexor Stretch

The student kneels with one knee and one foot flat on the floor, rocking gently forward until she feels the stretch on the top of her hip. She holds the stretch for fifteen seconds and then repeats it using the other leg.

Calf Stretch (Figure 8–9). Use the wall for support. Place palms on the wall and extend one leg directly behind until your toes barely touch the floor. Press down with the foot, trying to touch the heel to the floor. Hold the stretch for fifteen seconds, then relax and repeat with the other leg.

Figure 8-9
Calf Stretch
The student uses the wall for support and extends one leg behind until her toes barely touch the floor. She holds for fifteen seconds and then repeats the stretch using the other leg.

9
PREGNANCY AND OTHER PRACTICAL CONSIDERATIONS

Pregnancy

Sometimes female martial artists get pregnant. Can they continue martial arts practice? And what should you do as an instructor? Women who have exercised regularly before pregnancy can usually continue practicing during pregnancy (of course they should obtain the approval of their obstetrician first). They need to keep their workouts reasonable, however, and avoid arduous training. Routine exercise will not harm the child, and in fact can help the mother have an easier labor, a faster recovery, and more stamina throughout pregnancy and childbirth.

However, pregnancy is not the time to start taking a martial arts class. Women who have not been athletic or who have not participated in your class before becoming pregnant should be discouraged from doing so now. Invite them to sign up after the baby is born.

As the pregnancy progresses, your female student will need to modify what she can do. Certain women can still kick head high during the last trimester of pregnancy, but most cannot. Above all, encourage your pregnant student not to quit. Just have her slow down a bit. Remind her that once the baby is born she will get back to her former level of skill before long. She may even find that her skills have improved—her endurance certainly will.

You might feel more comfortable with a written or verbal confirmation from the student's physician that she can continue working out. This is not an unreasonable request to make. It can also help you clarify and understand what she can and cannot do during pregnancy.

Avoiding Injuries

Some general warnings apply for all pregnant women who plan to continue working out. Because of changes in the body during pregnancy, women are more easily injured during pregnancy than at any other time. Their weight distribution and center of gravity shift, which makes it more likely that they will lose their balance and fall. Since more pressure and stress is being put on their joints, overuse injuries, sprains, pulls, and tears are more common. The risk of injury can be reduced when the pregnant student moves more slowly, stretches carefully, and reduces the intensity of the workout.

High impact workouts should be avoided during pregnancy. Also, pregnant women should not lie on their backs. This restricts the flow of blood and oxygen to the fetus and the mother. This means avoiding crunches, leg lifts, or other such exercises. Of course, a pregnant woman should not lie on her stomach either. When your other students are doing push-ups and crunches, the pregnant woman can perform an alternative exercise, such as seated stretching or the like. Although many pregnant women find they have more flexibility, it is still very important for them to warm up, stretch, and cool down at each workout session.

Women who are pregnant may tire more easily. They should listen to their bodies. Now is not the time to push it. They should be allowed to take breaks when they need them, even if this is not normally encouraged in your classes. They should step out and sit down if they ever feel too warm, light-headed, or nauseated. They should not work out when it is extremely hot and humid. Feel free to ask your student any questions you may have about her pregnancy or her routine for working out during pregnancy.

Modifying the Workout

A pregnant martial artist should probably discontinue sparring as soon as she discovers she is pregnant. Although her baby is well protected by her body, it is best not to risk injury. She should also avoid throws and takedowns. This can put the pregnant practitioner at a disadvantage, but remember that everything can be modified. A pregnant judo student can still practice entering and breaking balance along with her partner without actually throwing each other to the mat.

Martial arts practice can be modified in a variety of ways. For instance, even if your tae kwon do student cannot do jumping kicks, she can still focus on the fundamentals such as the front kick, sidekick, and reverse kick. This will help her remain sharp and focused.

Maintaining Skills

The last few weeks of pregnancy and of childbirth itself are tiring experiences. Your martial arts student may not wish to continue her practice. Encourage her to keep thinking about martial arts even if she is not attending training sessions regularly. Give her ideas for keeping in shape during these weeks. For example, the new mother might be able to perform some stretches while her husband feeds the new baby. She might incorporate the baby in a workout that's light, short, and fun so that she maintains her flexibility and agility.

Most martial arts teach forms. Careful practice of these forms can help the woman in the late stages of pregnancy and after childbirth maintain her techniques and feel that she's still practicing the martial arts without exhausting herself.

You should encourage her to read about her martial arts discipline as she recovers. She can also learn about different styles. You might lend her some reading material or videotapes.

Try not to worry if she does not return to full speed right away. If possible, allow her to work out at about half speed until she feels completely recovered from childbirth. If she feels pressured to work out at her original intensity, she may put off returning to class for a longer period of time.

Most physicians recommend waiting six weeks after childbirth to start working out again. After a cesarean section, a longer recovery period is usually recommended. However, some women are able to return to class just a few weeks after childbirth. Either way, encourage the new mother to start working out again as soon as she feels ready and has her doctor's approval.

Some schools provide child care for newborns as well as older children while their parents work out. If this option is available, remind the new mother about it.

Menopause

Women experiencing other physical changes can continue to work out as well. At one time, women were discouraged from working out during and after menopause for fear of injury, but now the health-care profession encourages fitness programs for menopausal women. There's no reason a menopausal woman cannot continue her martial arts training. Of course, she may require some patience from you. The hormonal changes of menopause can sometimes cause women to be more emotional than usual. They may also find they are less flexible and may have more difficulty with stiffness and soreness. Simply be considerate of these concerns. Offer any information you have on maintaining flexibility and treating or avoiding muscle soreness or stiffness.

Menstruation

Women who are menstruating do not require any special consideration. There's no reason they cannot work out; in fact, physical exercise can make them feel better and can help reduce cramping and pain. Therefore, you don't need to worry about making any special accommodations for them.

Equipment and Clothing

One of the first things a female martial artist discovers is that almost all of the equipment—everything from practice uniforms to headgear—is actually made to fit men. This doesn't mean that good equipment for women does not exist, but it can be hard to find. It sometimes requires a lot of patience for female martial artists to find the gear they need. You can help out by keeping track of places that sell sporting equipment, especially martial arts equipment, for women.

You can also help by learning the female equivalent of male sizes, so that women can find the right fit when ordering uniforms and equipment. Inform small women that larger children's sizes may fit them.

Keep in mind that since uniforms are made to fit men, they can fit pretty strangely on women. Uniform tops that button or wrap are far more difficult for women to wear than uniform tops that slip over their heads. Consider allowing students to choose between wrap- and tunic-style tops. Also, pants for men are cut with similarly sized waists and hips. Because a woman's hips are larger than her waist, such pants can be difficult to wear: if she finds a pair to fit her hips, the waist is much too big; if a pair fits her waist, she can't get them over her hips. For these problems, consider drawstring or elastic-type pants that allow plenty of room for women to maneuver. Lace-up pants do not work very well for women.

Modifying Martial Arts Clothing

Uniforms and martial arts clothing can be modified by women to make them fit better. On uniform tops, darts can improve the fit. Additional snaps or Velcro closures on wrap-style tops can help them stay more securely closed. Darts in the back of pants can improve the fit too. For pants with too much elastic in the waist, the elastic can be cut to reduce its size and resewn. This will make the waist smaller.

Fitting Martial Arts Clothing and Uniforms

To help women select appropriate clothing sizes, keep the following guidelines available. Most karate-type uniforms are sold in a set of sizes, ranging from 000 to 7. The smallest children wear 000 and the biggest men wear 7. Both height and weight should be taken into account when selecting martial arts uniforms. Women who wear small sizes such as 8 and under and who are about 5'4" can fit into a size 3 uniform. Women up to 5'6" and 160 pounds can wear a size 4. This size works for women who wear a 10, 12, and 14 in women's clothing. Taller or heavier women will find a 5 a better bet.

Other martial arts clothing sold in men's sizes include sweat-shirts, T-shirts, and plain workout clothes. Men's sizes small, medium, and large are roughly equivalent to women's sizes medium, large, and extra large. However, because men's clothing fits more tightly across the chest, a woman who wears a large in women's clothing will often prefer a men's size large as well.

Shirts are often sized by collar size. Remember that men's clothes are more constricting than women's. A 17 or 17½ collar size will fit a size 14 woman. If she prefers a closer fit, she might be comfortable in a size 16½. A size 12 woman should be comfortable wearing a 15 or 16 collar.

Sometimes chest size is also indicated on men's clothing. For instance, a size 17½ collar might also indicate that it is for a size 36 chest. This is helpful for women; the chest size is usually equivalent to an average cup size. For instance, a men's 36 chest will fit a 36C woman, or one who wears a size 12 or 14. Smaller women can go down a chest size.

Men's pants may be sold in sizes such as 32 × 34. The first number indicates the waist in inches; the second is the length, or inseam size, in inches. These sizes are difficult for women to judge since their hips are usually much larger than their waists. Going by waist size may not yield the correct fit. For an average 5'5" woman who wears a size 12, a man's 32 × 30 is about right. Minor adjustments such as hemming may be needed. Size 34 × 32 pants will fit a size 14 or 16 woman who is taller (about 5'7" or so).

Fitting Sparring Equipment and Shoes

For sparring equipment, men's sizes are about one size larger than women's. Small gloves will work for the woman with medium-size hands. Foot gear is usually sold in small, medium, and large sizes. The medium will fit women who wear sizes 8 to 10. Small works for sizes 6 to 7½. Women who wear smaller sizes of shoes should wear larger children's shoe sizes.

Martial arts shoes (and sometimes foot gear) are sold by regular men's sizes, usually ranging from 3 to 13. Men's shoes are about a size and a half larger than women's. A woman who wears a size 9 shoe will probably be comfortable in the men's size 7½ or 8.

The actual size that works best will vary, but these measurements can show you where to begin. To make the process easier, simply note the size equivalents on a card, photocopy it, and distribute it to female students who plan to make equipment purchases.

10
Becoming a Female-Friendly Martial Arts School

One of the keys to maintaining a female-friendly environment is to encourage women to take martial arts classes. Retaining female students depends on whether they feel welcome in your school and in your classes.

Attracting Female Students

You can target women as potential students in a variety of ways. The way you advertise in the newspaper and on the radio is important. Emphasize concerns such as fitness and self-defense if you want to appeal to women. Further, if you use illustrations in your ads—such as a picture of your instructors or of a typical class—be sure they include women.

One way many martial arts instructors attract students to their school is by performing demonstrations. If you do this, include female martial artists in your demonstration and be certain that they share the spotlight. Girl Scout camps, sororities, and hospital nursing staffs are good audiences for whom you can demonstrate martial arts techniques. You can then distribute cards that are redeemable for a free class to encourage women to join your school.

Retaining Female Students

Is your school female friendly? The most important way to retain students—men and women—is to be a friendly, supportive school. If you have the opportunity to acquire female students, you should make an effort to keep them. Some schools offer women-only classes as a way to encourage women to sign up. This can be a good idea, especially for women who are hesitant or intimidated by working with men. But women should still be encouraged to work with men—realistically, that is the best way to learn how to defend themselves against men.

Encourage potential students to watch classes. This helps them become more comfortable about what happens in the class. Offer free introductory lessons in which you spend ten or fifteen minutes showing them the basic techniques and describing the basic expectations.

Any potential student has martial arts goals, although these aren't always clear to her. With your help, a potential student can identify her goals. If you show you care about what she wishes to achieve, she will be more interested in continuing her training with you.

Of course you must be honest. If your school emphasizes competition and winning sparring tournaments above all else, you must be frank about this with your students. You cannot expect them to stay with you if you promise them light contact and a cooperative environment when this is not the case.

Creating a Gender-Neutral Environment

A good martial arts teacher is committed to gender-neutral practices. You cannot allow male students to complain when they're assigned a female partner. Don't always pair women with women. Women at schools where women are treated differently from men do not stay.

One school expects women to do the same things as men, except women are not allowed to hold boards for board-breaking exercises. They're expected to break the boards, but they cannot hold them. This seems like a very silly and senseless gender division that reinforces the belief that women aren't very strong. It is just the kind of thing that will irritate female students and in the long run make them feel alienated and more likely to leave the school.

Another school routinely divides along gender lines when kicks are being practiced. Again, this is not a good idea. It communicates the belief that women aren't appropriate partners for men (and vice versa). It focuses too much attention on the students' gender.

My own experience in a gender-neutral school was very refreshing. It was the first place I had ever been where the fact that I was a woman made absolutely no difference. It simply wasn't relevant. What an empowering situation that was! The head instructor of the school insisted on gender-neutral practices. He may have had private opinions about women, but I never knew what they were. He was always impressed by his wife (who was assistant instructor), and he communicated his pride to his students. Students, male and female, believed they could achieve anything because of his good attitude.

Keeping Gender-Neutral Practices Consistent

Because the head instructor sets the tone for the school, it is important to set a gender-neutral tone. Do not allow assistant instructors to treat women differently than the way they treat men. Be certain to supervise any assistant instructors to make sure this is not happening. One assistant instructor can drive away a lot of female students in a school.

It is also a good idea to consider hiring female instructors. Frequently women are overlooked as potential teachers. But they can be some of the best teachers you'll ever have. The school that has at least one or two female instructors is more female friendly than one that does not.

Look around. Do you have several female black belts? If not, you may need to consider what you're doing wrong. If so, would any of them be interested in leading classes now and then? Cultivate their ability to teach and you'll have lifelong student-teachers.

Above all, be certain that you do not hold people to different standards. All students should be expected to do their best. This may differ from student to student, but you should not expect any less of women than you expect of men. This communicates itself to the class and is as bad as any sort of bias you could show. By attempting to become sensitive to the needs of your female students, you can help them learn martial arts, achieve their martial arts goals, and inspire excellent martial arts performance.